To Renee — May you find laughter, joyful tears, and FAITH in these pages! It was so great meeting a new sister in Christ and getting our nails done together!

Jesus

Oh How God Works…
When We Let Him

Be encou
Linda Bra ♡

Oh How God Works…
When We Let Him

Linda Brake

TATE PUBLISHING
AND **ENTERPRISES**, LLC

Oh How God Works... When We Let Him
Copyright © 2015 by Linda Brake. All rights reserved.

No part of this publication may be reproduced, stored in a retrieval system or transmitted in any way by any means, electronic, mechanical, photocopy, recording or otherwise without the prior permission of the author except as provided by USA copyright law.

This book is designed to provide accurate and authoritative information with regard to the subject matter covered. This information is given with the understanding that neither the author nor Tate Publishing, LLC is engaged in rendering legal, professional advice. Since the details of your situation are fact dependent, you should additionally seek the services of a competent professional.

The opinions expressed by the author are not necessarily those of Tate Publishing, LLC.

Published by Tate Publishing & Enterprises, LLC
127 E. Trade Center Terrace | Mustang, Oklahoma 73064 USA
1.888.361.9473 | www.tatepublishing.com

Tate Publishing is committed to excellence in the publishing industry. The company reflects the philosophy established by the founders, based on Psalm 68:11,
"The Lord gave the word and great was the company of those who published it."

Book design copyright © 2015 by Tate Publishing, LLC. All rights reserved.
Cover design by Ivan Charlem Igot
Interior design by Richell Balansag
Front cover and author photo by Jamie Herrera Photography

Published in the United States of America

ISBN: 978-1-68164-168-3
1. Religion / Christian Life / General
2. Biography & Autobiography / Personal Memoirs
15.05.29

Contents

Prologue 7
Adam 9
Alexis 13
Quarter Carat Miracle 17
Brought Together by an Angel 19
The Perfect Job 25
Born Again 27
Take Up Your Cross 33
Together at Last 37
Be Healed 39
Make Him or Break Him 41
The Baseball Bat 43
Out of the Mouths of Babes 45
Fine, I'll Say the Prayer 47
God's Amazing Love 51
One Fateful Saturday 53
Cold Turkey 59
That Was Stupid 61
Special Forces Angel 63
It's Not the TV 65
Tithe? Are You Crazy? 67

Do You Need a Job?	69
Pepper	71
Fred	73
Mom's Homecoming	75
Heinz	81
Dad's Homecoming	83
Lady	85
Saving the Gym	87
Calvary Chapel Pagosa Springs	93
Be Careful What You Pray For	95
Jean	97
Anonymous Angel	101
How Will People Know?	103
My Demon	105
Chris	113
Madison	115
Booker	117
Too Much Fun	121
Covering My Mistakes	123
God's Plans—Not Mine	125
Oh, How God Works When We Let Him	129
The Roman Road	133

Prologue

I never thought about being a writer, I never wanted to write a book, and I never took any writing classes. But I have lots of stories about God that I love to share, and lots of times, people have told me that I should write a book. A number of thoughts had come to my mind, causing me to pause and think that maybe I should write this book.

In the chapter entitled "Take Up Your Cross," God told me to share my story to a small group of people at a singles retreat. If he wanted me to share then, why wouldn't he want me to share to the whole world?

If you talk to every other Christian in the whole wide world about how God has answered their prayers, I'm sure they would have stories that top mine. Multiply my stories by a gazillion, and that's how God answers prayers and how he works in any Christian's life. How are my stories more special than any other Christian's? They're not. I'm just one who wrote a book about them.

What if just one person got saved because of my book? What if one person was encouraged by my book? Why, it would be worth every penny and ounce of effort I spent writing it! To God be the glory!

Besides, I was watching an episode of *Castle* one night. He was speaking to an elementary school class, and one of the students raised her hand and asked him if she could be a writer. Castle returned with a question, "Can you tell a story?" She said that she could. He said, "Then you can write a book." Well, that cinched it. If Richard Castle says I can write a book, then I guess I can!

I am an only child raised in a home with a couple of Bibles lying around. I have no recollection of either my mom or dad actually reading them. In fact, I remember Mom telling me the Bible was just a collection of fairytales. None of them are true. Well, that was just one of the fairytales she told me. I have found through experience that if there's one thing I can count on from God, it's the truth.

This book is a collection of answered prayers from my life. Some might say that answered prayers are no more than coincidences. William Temple was a bishop in the Church of England 1881–1944. He would then reply, "When I pray, coincidences happen. When I don't, they don't."

If you're one of the scoffers, I would challenge you to read the answered prayers here and tell me they're just coincidences. My hope is that you will find, as I have, that God is always true to his word, and he answers prayers as long as we trust him to take the wheel.

If you are a believer, my desire is that the answered prayers in this little book will lift your spirits and give you encouragement.

Adam

September 1982

By the time I was in my late twenties, I was fixed firmly in my mother's ideas about God and the Bible. A young man in his teens came up to me in the Albertson's parking lot and attempted to hand me a tract. I rudely rebuked him, threw his tract at him, got into my car, and drove away. I hope he didn't give up because of me. In all my life, he was the only stranger who ever tried to witness to me.

I married an atheist when I was nineteen. After several years, I decided that it was time to start a family. After two more years, it was time to see a doctor.

After checking my husband out and being told he was fine, it was my turn to be examined. The doctor found a flap beside my cervix that was indicative of having been exposed to a hormone called diethylstilbestrol, DES for short. From about 1940 to 1971, DES was given to pregnant women with the mistaken belief it would reduce the risk of pregnancy complications and losses. I called my mother, and she confirmed that she had been given this drug during the first trimester of her pregnancy with me, and so I indeed had been exposed. This drug was banned by the FDA because it caused sterility in female offspring, among other things. The doctor suggested that I undergo a hysterosalpingogram to see if there was any blockage in my fallopian tubes before declaring me sterile.

As I drove home, I looked up to the sky and said, "God, if you'll give me a baby boy, I will raise him as a Christian." (I really have no idea why I prayed that.) I endured the test a couple of weeks later, and no blockage was found. The doctor gave me the fatal news that he believed I was sterile.

About five weeks later, I was feeling sick to my stomach. I visited my doctor's office again only to find out that I was pregnant! At that time, my prayer came back to mind. I asked my doctor, "Is there any way that test blew something out of my fallopian tubes?" He replied, "No. In fact, it's a miracle that you're pregnant. If you had conceived before the test, we would have blown the baby away, so you then had to have conceived within two days after." Frankly, after the trouble I had having that test done, I can't imagine my baby being conceived that soon afterward. Well, without going into more detail, I was convinced that God performed a miracle in me.

Adam Tyler was born September 19, 1982.

> Then God remembered Rachel, and God listened to her and opened her womb. And she conceived and bore a son. (Gen. 30:22)

I remembered my prayer after I had been home for a couple of months and had sufficiently recovered from my delivery. My next-door neighbor went to a Presbyterian church, about fifteen minutes away, so I decided I would take Adam and drop him off at the nursery and go home. After dropping him off, I thought about it and decided that the sermon couldn't take longer than an hour. And by the time I drove home and came back, that would only leave me half an hour. Oh, what the heck! I guess I'll go see what the minister has to say.

Alexis

September 1984

During the delivery of my son, because of my exposure to DES, I hemorrhaged. I lost four pints of blood and almost died on the delivery table. So needless to say, I was a little hesitant about having a second child. Being an only child myself and hating not having a brother or sister, I visited several ob-gyns to see who might be willing to do a C-section on me should I be able to conceive another child. I found a wonderful doctor on my fifth try who agreed to do a C-section, but simply asked that I wait to make my decision. I again looked up at the sky and asked God if I could have a little girl, and I'd like my children to be two years apart since I had heard siblings would grow up closer to each other if they were not separated by too many years. My second miracle baby was conceived, and the doctor estimated the due date to be the same day as Adam's, two years later.

Our pastor had left the little Presbyterian church where I was attending, and they had hired an interim pastor, Dr. Serviss. We were talking one day, and I told Dr. Serviss that I felt I was going to die while delivering this child. He assured me I would not die. He said he had been praying for me and sensed God telling him I would be okay.

Five weeks after conception, I began to bleed, and upon examination, my doctor explained that all the old tears had opened up again, and I would have to be on bed rest the entire pregnancy. It would prove to be one of the most difficult times of my life.

After about five months, it was time for an ultrasound to check on the baby. I wanted a baby girl so bad, especially since I knew this would be my last. The ultrasound picture was not definitive, but the technician said she thought I might be having another son. I was driven home and put back to bed. As I laid there staring up at the ceiling with tears rolling in my ears, I said, "Surely, you wouldn't put me through this and not give me a little girl?"

As my time to deliver drew near, I began to bleed again. We called my doctor who instructed us to get in to the hospital immediately. When we arrived, I was given a "saddle block" and was lying on the delivery table waiting for the doctor. My doctor walked in and said that it was a good thing the baby had not come while we were on our way because I would have bled to death before help could arrive. She nonchalantly said, "You know, Dr. Walker and I really didn't think you would be able to keep this baby."

Alexis Deanne was born by C-section two years and four days after her brother.

The next morning, Dr. Varma burst into my room and asked me excitedly if I had been having stomach pains prior to my C-section. I told her, as a matter of fact, I was in severe pain, but the nurse felt it was just gas. Dr. Varma explained to me that when she had cut into my abdomen, my appendix was "red hot" and she had to remove it. If it had burst, I could have died.

> For your Father knows things you have need of before you ask Him. (Matt. 6:8)

Quarter Carat Miracle

January 1985

I had heard the warnings to never leave your baby in a carrier on top of a table. But I thought it would be fine. I was just inside the kitchen doing dishes, where I could keep an eye on her.

All of a sudden, I heard a crash. Alexis had wrestled herself out of her chair, rolled off the table, and promptly landed on the floor. I sometimes wonder how either one of my children survived my parenting. I ran and gathered her up to check her for any injury. She settled right down, and I laid her carefully on her blanket on the floor. It was a busy day. I finished the dishes and did the laundry when I felt for the diamond in my wedding ring as I often did throughout my waking hours. Hmmm. It felt different. I looked at the setting where my diamond was no longer attached. Oh no! I had lost my diamond! I was devastated!

I thought back through my day and knew my diamond could be down the kitchen drain or out through the washing machine hose. With despair, I began to retrace my steps, trying to look for a needle in a haystack.

After about an hour of searching frantically, I was crawling across the living room floor, scouring every inch of it when I decided to stop. Then I knelt down and cried out to Jesus, "Lord, you know where my diamond is! Please, oh please, could you help me find it?"

Almost immediately, I found myself crawling in a straight line directly into the dining room to the area where I had picked Alexis up off the floor. I looked down to see a tiny little pebble in the carpet. I picked it up and turned it over in my hand. It was my diamond!

> Or what woman, having ten silver coins, if she loses one coin, does not light a lamp, sweep the house, and search carefully until she finds it? And when she has found it, she calls her friends and neighbors together, saying, "Rejoice with me, for I have found the piece which I lost!" Likewise, I say to you, there is joy in the presence of the angels of God over one sinner who repents. (Luke 15:8–10)

Brought Together by an Angel

September 1985

While still in my tumultuous marriage with my children's father, I was attending the same Presbyterian church where I had started my spiritual journey. Upon realizing my marriage was failing and I seemed to be the only one wanting to save it, I began counseling with Dr. Serviss at the same time that I was attending marriage counseling with my half-hearted husband.

Dr. Serviss gave me some advice that I am happy that I followed to this day. He said, "Before going through with a divorce, you must do everything in your power, with fervent prayer, to save your marriage. Only when you have tried everything and it is so bad that you can honestly say, even if he turned himself around, you could not be with him, then and only then should you even consider a divorce." And let me also preface this, without going into detail, that there were very serious issues. Divorce should never be considered lightly.

Then began four months of intensive counseling and my goal of staying in my marriage. But instead of improving matters, our relationship went from bad to worse. And

Sunday mornings were the worst. As I would get the kids ready for church, my husband distanced himself emotionally, farther and farther away from me.

One Sunday in September of 1985, I went to counseling with my pastor. I was in a terrible funk and told him I had decided that all men are shallow and selfish, and I never wanted anything to do with another man for the rest of my life. My pastor replied, "You are correct in part. However, there are a few men who have been through what you have been through and want the same kind of relationship you want."

I asked him how I would know this "gem" when I found him. He told me to go very slow and make a list of my needs in a new relationship and to tick them off one by one. And if I found any negative traits, I should decide if I can tolerate them, because I would never be able to change him.

He then told me a story of when he was a chaplain at an Indian reservation. He said that once in a while, one of the Indians would try to get off the reservation. He would have to travel three days through a desert with no water. My pastor would go out with the tribal officer to find the escapee. When they found him, they would give him water literally one drop at a time, or it would kill him. He then said I had been through a long, hot desert in ten years of marriage without a drop of love. If I went too fast in a new relationship, it could literally kill me.

As I drove home, I looked up at the clouds again and said, "Lord, if there's a man like that out there for me, I would really like to meet him." I was thinking to myself a couple of years down the road.

The next Sunday, I found an ad on the church bulletin board for square dancing lessons. I was thinking that my husband and I had not been out on a date, and we had no interests in common anymore. What if we took square dancing lessons? I hurried home, excited to tell him. Unfortunately, he flat out refused. At our next appointment, our counselor suggested I go without him. Red flags immediately sprang up in my mind, and I wondered, *What kind of advice is that?* But I told our counselor and my husband that I would do just that.

The following Tuesday, September 17, I was at class as the lesson was about to start when Wanda walked in. She's the lady who had posted the ad at my church. With her was a handsome man, about my age. I walked up to greet Wanda, and she introduced me to Arty. Having been an only child and never around the opposite sex much, I always felt very awkward around men. Weirdly, I was able to talk with Arty as if he were a long lost brother. I immediately began to grow very fascinated with him, and I felt a strong attraction.

Wanda partnered with Arty. Out of a class of twenty-two couples, there were only two other singles—another young man and myself. They partnered me up with the other single gentleman.

While driving home, I grew steadily more afraid, asking myself, "What in the world are you doing?" I went home and begged my husband to go to the next class with me. They even offered to let him in free of charge for the first couple of classes. My husband again refused. I told him I would get down on my knees and kiss his feet if he would at least try and go with me. He still flatly refused. So I said, "Well, there's a nice-looking single dad there. Maybe I'll just see if I can get something going with him." My husband looked at me with disdain and said he really didn't care what I did.

What I did not know at the time was that Arty actually lived next to Wanda. He had been recovering from a nasty divorce for two years and had gone into a deep depression. One day, he saw Wanda come home in her square dancing outfit and decided he had been moping around long enough. He also had been praying that God would bring a woman into his life with two kids who he could help out with. (I have no idea why he prayed that.) He ran out to greet Wanda and said he wanted to get out and learn how to square dance. He and Wanda showed up the next Tuesday for class.

The second Tuesday, Wanda's work schedule changed, and she was no longer able to accompany Arty. My previous partner never showed up again either. They only had two singles now, so naturally, they partnered Arty with me.

A couple of months later during class, I was hurt and angry and at the end of my rope with my husband who still was not motivated to work on our relationship. I told Arty everything that night and said that I was giving up. He took me by the shoulders, looked me straight in the eyes, and said, "If you ever thought about starting a relationship with me, you promise me you'll go back home and give your husband another chance first!"

I did go back home that night and tried again and again. I left home with my children over the Thanksgiving weekend and never looked back.

Arty and I were married two years later.

So how does that angel get into the picture? Well, in square dancing classes, experienced dancers will fill in a square or partner with a single student. These experienced dancers are called angels. Wanda was our angel.

Oh, and about that list to match up to that gem of a man? Arty met all my requests and even one I had not thought to add. The man can dance.

> If you then, being evil, know how to give good gifts to your children, how much more will your Father who is in heaven give good things to those who ask Him! (Matt. 7:11)

What seemed like a fairytale turned into a fifteen-year nightmare. Our children suffered, and we suffered. Please, if you're considering divorce and you have children, for their sake, do everything to save your marriage. God really does know best.

But did He not make them one, having a remnant of the Spirit? And why one? He seeks godly offspring. Therefore take heed to your spirit, and let none deal treacherously with the wife of his youth. "For the Lord God of Israel says that He hates divorce, for it covers one's garment with violence," says the Lord of hosts. (Mal. 2:15–16)

The Perfect Job

November 1985

One thing I learned from Dr. Serviss is that the opposite of love is not hate. The opposite of love is indifference. Boy, did I ever learn that the hard way. When it became clear that my marriage was not going to make it no matter how hard I tried to save it, I began making plans to move on as a single parent. Again, forgetting to pray and striking out on my own, I contacted an employment agency. They placed me at an accounting firm as a bookkeeper, and I quickly learned this was a company where I just couldn't fit in.

God is so gracious. He will never force himself on you even though he knows he could do a much better job at everything. Sometimes, I wish he wasn't so darned polite.

This time, I prayed before contacting a temp agency. I said, "Lord, now that I can't spend as much time with my precious children, do you think you could provide a job for me with shorter hours? And maybe good benefits would be important. And gee, it sure would be nice to have a short commute. Oh, and I don't think I'm really in the mood for working with a lot of people. Would it be possible for me to just have a job where I can sit in a nice, quiet cubicle and type all day? Okay. Well, I think that's all. Thanks."

That week the agency sent me on a temporary assignment at the Arabian Horse Registry as a transcriptionist sitting in a cubicle, typing all day. They offered me full-time employment and I accepted. It had great benefits and a decent pay. Plus, it had a seven-hour work day and was only ten minutes from my new apartment.

It was perfect.

> So why do you worry about clothing? Consider the lilies of the field, how they grow; they neither toil nor spin; and yet I say to you that even Solomon in all his glory was not arrayed like one of these. Now if God so clothes the grass of the field, which today is, and tomorrow is thrown into the oven, will He not much more clothe you, O you of little faith? Therefore do not worry, saying, "What shall we eat?" or "What shall we drink?" or "What shall we wear?" For after all these things the Gentiles seek. For your heavenly Father knows that you need all these things. But seek first the kingdom of God and His righteousness, and all these things shall be added to you. Therefore do not worry about tomorrow, for tomorrow will worry about its own things. Sufficient for the day is its own trouble. (Matt. 6:28–34)

Born Again

September 1986

After my divorce and while experiencing single parenting firsthand, I found myself churchless. I prayed, "Lord, I need a church where I will get good teaching. Please send me to the church where you want me to be."

The next morning, my radio alarm woke me up to an advertisement about a divorce recovery workshop being held that weekend at Faith Presbyterian Church, thirty-seven miles away from my home. At the workshop, I was handed a brochure for a singles retreat. Now, you must understand that I am a Type A personality. I don't keep anything around that I'm not interested in. And I was definitely not interested in spending a weekend away from my kids. Besides, I certainly didn't feel that I had the $40 required for the retreat.

I arrived back home, and somehow, that brochure ended up on my microwave instead of in the trash. Every time I passed by the microwave, I'd stop and ponder on going to the retreat, then promptly shake my head and walk away.

About two weeks before the retreat, I filled out the brochure and wrote a check. All the while, it felt like my hand was moving on its own accord as I asked myself, "What are you doing?" I placed the brochure with the check in the mail and promptly asked my supervisor if I could have time off that Friday.

Monday morning before the retreat, I jabbed myself in the gums with my toothbrush. By Friday, I was in so much pain that I had to see my dentist. I then called his number, hoping and praying I could get in with such late notice. I was surprised when the assistant said, "If you can come now, it's his only available appointment all day." I told her I would be there in ten minutes. After examining me, my dentist said, "You have an abscessed canker sore." He put some medicine on it and told me that it wouldn't feel much better by Monday, but if there was no improvement, I should come back in.

I then left for the retreat, which was being held in beautiful Westcliffe, Colorado, grumbling to myself and wondering why I was going to this thing. When I reached Colorado Springs, I felt a relief pour over me, and laughter came from my innermost being and expanded into giggling for absolutely no reason at all. I thought, *Well, I guess God wants me to go!*

This was before the days of GPS, so of course I got lost. It was ten at night when I arrived, registered, and entered a dark cabin with a flashlight to get settled in. My canker sore was killing me. I didn't know anyone there. As I lay in the bottom bunk—hate the bottom bunk—a dark cloud of depression began to cover me. I quietly cried myself to sleep.

When I arose the next morning, the dark cloud of depression had become thicker and felt evil. I began going through the motions, ate breakfast, listened to the speaker, and we broke up into predetermined groups. As I sat there with five other ladies, our leader, Rich, said that he wanted everyone to introduce themselves and describe what they expected to gain from this retreat.

I thought frantically, *I don't even know why I'm here! I don't want to be here!* Of course, Rich started with the lady to his right and I was on his left, which made me last. I listened to the other five describe their hopes for the weekend, one by one. They all had such wonderful things to say. I started to panic even more. I had nothing to say! Then it was my turn. I burst out crying, the dark cloud becoming blacker and thicker, enveloping my very soul. Rich said, "I think this lady needs hands laid on her." Well, I had never heard of that before. Rich asked me if it was okay. I was crying so hard, all I could do was shrug my shoulders and nod my head. They all gathered around me and laid hands on me and began to pray. Rich began to speak in a strange language. I thought, *Oh my God! I'm in a cult!* But at the same time, I felt the darkness recede and I was able to stop crying and calmed down.

Rich then explained that the Holy Spirit had spoken to him and said they were all there to minister to me. I found out later that everyone there was already born again, except me. Rich then told me the Holy Spirit had not given him any other specifics, so they were going to start asking me questions.

As I was answering questions about my family and circumstances, the lady next to me, Patti, grabbed my knee and asked, "Are you born again?"

I said smugly, "I'm a Christian."

"Have you said the prayer?"

I said even more arrogantly, "I've said many prayers."

Patti then explained that if I had said this prayer, I would know what she was talking about.

I looked at her and then said, "Okay, so what's your prayer?"

"It's just simply a prayer where you admit you're a sinner and ask God into your heart to be your Lord and Savior."

I said, "If you think it will help." I repeated the prayer with her and everyone was so excited for me.

As I walked out, Suzie walked up alongside me asking, "Are you okay?"

"I don't feel any different."

She said, "You don't have to. Jesus is inside you now, changing you from the inside out. You don't have to white-knuckle it anymore."

That phrase resonated with me immediately because that was exactly what I had been doing. I had no purpose, no reason to even be alive. I had so many questions and no answers. Life had no meaning, and it seemed like no matter how hard I tried, nothing ever turned out for me.

As I lay down for the night, I noticed that all of a sudden my canker sore didn't hurt anymore.

The next morning, I went down to the main lodge for breakfast. As I passed Rich and Patti sitting on the porch (as Patti reported to me later), they watched me walk by with a little light following behind me.

Patti turned to Rich and asked, "Is she okay?"

Rich replied, "Oh yeah. She's going to be just fine now."

After breakfast, as I stepped out onto the porch again, I looked up into a stand of gorgeous Ponderosa pines, and they were literally sparkling. As I stared and stared at them, I realized I was seeing with such clarity, something I had never experienced before. I was actually seeing in three dimensions. I had never felt such peace. I'm actually not very sure of how I drove home. I don't really remember the journey at all. But one thing I realized, I guess God really did want me to go to that retreat. From then on even up until now, every time I see a stand of ponderosas, I look at them carefully and remember back to that wonderful experience.

I remembered my friend Mary from back when I first met my husband. She was a strong Christian, and I knew she attended church. So of course, she was the first one I called to tell the news. I exclaimed to her, "Mary, I'm born again!" She didn't seem the least bit surprised, didn't miss a beat, laughed, and just replied, "Well, it's about time. I've been praying for you for eight years!"

> Jesus answered, "Most assuredly, I say to you, unless one is born of water and the Spirit, he cannot enter the kingdom of God. That which is born of the flesh is flesh, and that which is born of the Spirit is Spirit. Do not marvel that I said to you "You must be born again." The wind blows where it wishes, and you hear the sound of it, but cannot tell where it comes from and where it goes. So is everyone who is born of the Spirit." (John 3:5–8)

After attending the retreat, I knew of course this was the church I had prayed for. I began attending regularly with Adam and Alexis. One Sunday as we drove to church, I was listening to a message on a local Christian station, and I said, "Lord, I know Faith is a great church, but isn't there somewhere closer?" At that very moment the pastor said, "You know, it's like the lady who gets her hair done clear across town because she doesn't trust anyone else to do it right, but she goes to the church around the corner because it's close." Well, I guess that settled that.

Take Up Your Cross

January 1987

After seeing Arty on a daily basis, I forgot all that Dr. Serviss told me about going slow. I threw caution to the wind and jumped in with both feet. Poor Arty didn't know what hit him. We were still square dancing every Tuesday night, and I just decided that was our night together. Of course, by that time, I had convinced Arty that it was okay. God knew we were committed to each other. Mom and Dad kept the kids overnight anyway, so why not?

> Now the serpent was more cunning than any beast of the field. (Gen. 3:1)
>
> So the woman took of its fruit and ate. She also gave to her [boyfriend] with her, and he ate. (Gen. 3:6)

I began to feel like there was an angel sitting on my right shoulder and the devil on my left. The angel was shaking her finger at me and scolding me, and the devil was coaxing me on. I just kept flicking that angel off my shoulder.

January came time for another singles retreat. I signed myself up and invited Arty again, but he still didn't want to join me. It was time to head up the mountain again, and when I arrived, Suzie and Mark were already there. Suzie immediately noticed I wasn't myself and asked if I felt okay. I told her I was feeling a little blah. She said, "Let's pray." She and Mark laid hands on me and began to pray. When they finished, Suzie asked if I felt any better. I told her I did not, so they laid hands on me and prayed again. As they were praying, Suzie said, "Lord, please reveal Linda's sin to her so she can be in perfect communion with you once again."

Oh, boy! I knew exactly what sin Suzie was talking about. I became belligerent and stubborn, telling God we weren't hurting anyone and only had one night a week. I refused to give it up. Right then, it felt as though God turned around in his chair so that his back was to me. He never left me. He just made his opinion crystal clear. Again, I felt that same darkness begin to fall down upon me but still I refused to repent.

By the next morning, I was in a terrible, dark place, and I felt Satan was knocking at my door. His presence was palpable. I had fallen so far from God's grace, but I was still unwilling to turn around even though I was scared out of my wits. I spent Saturday falling farther and farther into the abyss.

Then it was time for our Sunday church service. As I listened to Pastor Fred, I finally came to the place of surrender. I began to sob uncontrollably and began crying out, "Jesus help me!" Over and over, I pleaded and cried as everyone around me began laying hands on me and interceding on my behalf.

After a few minutes, I was finally able to calm myself down. As my friends were still praying, I had my head in my hands, bowed down to my knees, and closed my eyes, when all of a sudden, I saw a cross with a form on it. It looked as if I had opened my eyes and saw a bright window, and then closed my eyes to see the window reflected on my eyelids. So I opened my eyes and looked all around the room for something I might have looked at. There were no crosses anywhere.

I closed my eyes again, and this time, two empty crosses appeared on either side of it. I knew, of course, that the center cross was Jesus, hanging there for my sin. And I also knew the one empty cross was there for me to take up. So I said that I would gladly take up my cross now. But why was the other cross there? I sensed God wanted me to share with the group. I turned to Joy, sitting next to me, and told her that I needed to share something. She passed a note to Pastor Fred as he finished presenting the communion.

When everyone had partaken, Pastor Fred opened up the floor for me. I admitted my sin to everyone there and explained about my vision up until the point where I did not understand about the second empty cross.

At that moment, the gentleman speaking at the retreat said the second empty cross meant that there was someone else who needed to share. At that moment, another couple stood up and admitted that they were engaged but had become intimate. She cried and bowed her head. All of a sudden, she exclaimed, "I see a hill with hundreds, no thousands of empty crosses!"

I closed my eyes and saw her vision, too. I cried, "I see them, too!"

I left the retreat and went directly to Arty's home to break the news. Shortly after, the engaged couple announced they were getting married the next month instead of waiting a year as they had planned.

> Marriage is honorable among all, and the bed undefiled; but fornicators and adulterers God will judge. (Heb. 13:4)
>
> When He had called the people to Himself, with His disciples also, He said to them, "Whoever desires to come after Me, let him deny himself, and take up his cross, and follow Me. For whoever desires to save his life will lose it, but whoever loses his life for My sake and the gospel's will save it." (Mark 8:34–35)

Together at Last

December 1987

After we were married in November of 1987, Arty and his daughter Megan were still attending their Baptist church in Westminster while Adam, Alexis, and I were attending Faith Presbyterian Church in Aurora. Then, Adam and Alexis, who were five and three years of age, decided that they didn't want to drive all the way to Aurora. Arty and Megan were spending two hours while our trip made our Sunday mornings a full four hours. The coup was accomplished, and I found myself driving to Aurora from Thornton all by myself.

No amount of coaxing would bend the will of the rest of my family. I began to get frustrated and hurt. I knew God had called me to Faith. How could I convince my family that there was a good reason for that? I cajoled and begged and bribed—I did everything, except pray. My frustration was turning into anger, and Sundays were becoming cumbersome.

Finally, I came to my senses and threw up my hands, telling God I was done. If he wanted Arty and the kids to come to church with me in Aurora, then it was up to him to make that happen.

The next Sunday, Arty told me he had decided he and the kids were going to visit Faith with me. I stared at him with my mouth open. We went to church together. It was wonderful to be there as a family.

And the next Sunday, they announced their semiannual membership class. Arty signed up immediately. We spent the next thirteen years there together as a family.

> Every kingdom divided against itself is brought to desolation, and every city or house divided against itself will not stand. (Matt. 12:25)

Be Healed

November 1988

When Alexis was three, I was putting her to bed one night and happened to look at her right wrist. I noticed raised, wart-like bumps in a wavy line going up her arm. I had never seen anything like that before. I made an appointment the next day to have her arm examined by a dermatologist.

The doctor looked at them and explained that they were a delayed birthmark. He said that it was quite common but unfortunately unsightly. They would continue to go up her arm until she was possibly in her early teens. He suggested I bring her back then, when they had stopped spreading, and he would perform surgery to remove them.

Well, why wait? I figured it wouldn't hurt to ask the Lord to heal her. It's up to him if he wants to do it for us, but I certainly won't know if I don't ask. So, I was putting her to bed that night, and I laid my hand on the bumps and just asked God to please remove them.

I actually forgot all about them and my prayer until a couple of weeks later. I remembered and looked at her arm just to see if they were gone—and they were! There were no signs of them, even now.

(Jesus) bore our sins in His own body on the tree, that we, having died to sins, might live for righteousness—by whose stripes you were healed. (1 Pet. 2:24)

Make Him or Break Him

March 1989

When I first met Arty and into the second year of our marriage, he owned his own business. It was a small excavating company. He had an old dump truck and a backhoe and employed his brother and a couple of other laborers. He was struggling and barely making ends meet. The first two years we were married, when we did our taxes, we found that we owed four thousand dollars. The first year was bad enough, but the second did me in.

I had a discussion with God and asked him to please make or break Arty's business. In my mind, I was hoping God would make him. Why I didn't just pray that God would help him be successful is beyond me. Either I just don't think things through very well or God directed my prayer, because in the end, it turned out to be in our best interests.

We also had just registered and paid for a marriage seminar that was being held at a mega church on the west side of town. We were to attend the seminar the next weekend.

During the four days following my prayer, a number of things happened: First, Arty received a letter from his insurance agent notifying him that the premium for the liability insurance on his company had doubled. Second, he received a letter from the State of Colorado informing him that his payroll taxes had increased. On Friday, both his dump truck and his backhoe broke down. He came home totally discouraged and so depressed he didn't want to go to the seminar.

I convinced him that we needed to go to the seminar, especially since we had already paid for it, and also because God may want him there. I felt terrible about my earlier prayer and began praying fervently that the Lord would have someone there who could encourage Arty and lift his spirits.

We entered the church that Saturday morning. It was huge. I had never seen anything like it. There must have been thousands of couples in attendance. We walked down an aisle and found two empty seats. We weren't sitting there long before Arty started staring at the gentleman seated directly in front of us. Arty looked and looked and then finally he exclaimed, "Donnie?" The man turned around and recognized Arty right away. They were old friends who had not seen each other since junior high school!

> But You, O Lord, are a shield for me, My glory and the One who lifts up my head. I cried to the Lord with my voice, and He heard me from His holy hill. (Ps. 3:3)

The Baseball Bat

April 1989

I had always loved telling jokes and making people laugh. I don't have the quick sense of humor Arty has, so I have to manufacture it. My jokes were sometimes what I would call cute, dirty jokes. You know, the ones that don't cross the line into raunchy.

I noticed that angel was back, sitting on my right shoulder, trying to let me know gently that my cute, dirty jokes were apparently not as cute as I thought. But again, I was not listening. I told God he was going to have to use a baseball bat or a brick or a two-by-four or something if he wanted me to stop. I wasn't going to get it any other way. I just couldn't see the harm of it.

My friend Sue called a couple of days later and asked me to meet her and a friend for drinks, and I told her I would. Drinks for me involve a soda, glass of tea, or water. I had learned in my early twenties that drinking alcohol in abundance just causes me problems. The lesson happened one day after I apparently took a swing at my then father-in-law and couldn't remember the incident. I decided pretty quickly I would rather be in control of me rather than the demon drink.

So off to the bar I went to meet Sue and her friend. Her friend and I immediately started trading jokes—my cute, dirty jokes and his raunchy jokes. We had a good time as I kept catching Sue out of the corner of my eye with her jaw dropped onto the table. An hour or so later, Sue's friend had to leave, so we said our farewells.

Sue immediately lit into me. She asked me, "Do you not remember me telling you about this man?"

I replied, "No, Sue, I don't."

She reminded me that she had told me of this man she had met and that he was the owner of a topless bar. Sue had been trying to bear witness to him and told him to come meet a really nice Christian woman.

> But beware lest somehow this liberty of yours become a stumbling block to those who are weak. (1 Cor. 9:9)

Out of the Mouths of Babes

May 1989

After my conversion, I was burdened to pray that my loved ones and friends would find the love of Jesus and ask him into their hearts. I fervently prayed for them, especially for my mother.

One Saturday, while the kids were with their dad, I figured I had several hours to go convince my mom. I used every tool in my toolbox but to no avail. After listening to me for two hours, her response was, "Well, if that's what I have to do, then I'd rather go to hell!" I left tired and disappointed.

The next weekend, Mom and Dad were at our house for their weekly visit. The boys were downstairs watching a football game while Alexis, Mom, and I were sitting around the table, playing cards.

Suddenly, Alexis said, "Grandma, I want you to go to heaven with me. Please, won't you say the prayer?" Mom looked at Alexis and said immediately that she would love to say the prayer. Alexis, at the tender age of four, couldn't remember how it went, so I started line by line. Alexis repeated it, and then her grandma repeated after her.

Immediately upon returning home, Mom got her Bible off the shelf, dusted it off, and started reading. But I wanted her so much to find the teaching and fellowship that only a good church can provide. I began praying.

In the meantime, I thought I'd give God a hand by taking Mom to several churches in her neighborhood. After exhausting our short list, we were unable to find a suitable church. I still had not learned that God does not need my help.

Shortly after I gave up, Mom was taking a walk, and as she approached a Presbyterian church a couple of miles from her house, there was a lady trimming the roses out front who began a conversation with her and invited her to church.

Mom attended the church every Sunday and helped put together the bulletins every week until she went home to be with our Lord.

> And they continued steadfastly in the apostles' doctrine and fellowship, in the breaking of bread, and in prayers. (Acts 2:42)

Fine, I'll Say the Prayer

June 1989

After Mom was saved, that left Dad. He had grown up in the Lutheran church, but he had left when he was fourteen and never looked back. He was so bitter he wouldn't even come to my little Presbyterian church when I had the kids baptized. I knew I would have to tread carefully.

I began to just share the subjects that my pastor spoke about at Faith, trying to steer clear of any references that would indicate that I didn't think Dad was a Christian, even though I knew he was not saved. One day, he had enough. He blew up at me, literally spitting, as his angry words came out at me. "How dare you insinuate that I'm not a Christian!" he screamed. I was so taken aback by it since I had not said anything that would even hint at that. I left shaken and hurt.

I called my friend Mary. She told me that Satan had him in his grasp. "You don't think he's going to let go that easily, do you? And you must have hit a nerve and at least he's thinking about it."

I went back to visit him the next Sunday after church, undaunted and ready to share my pastor's message again.

My dad told me he didn't want to hear it anymore. I told him that if he would pray with me, then I would promise not to say another word. To my surprise, Dad agreed. I thought how unorthodox that was as I shook my head, wondering if it would even mean anything. But I had opened my big mouth, so I was going to keep my word regardless.

I began the prayer, "Jesus, I'm a sinner."

Dad said, "Of course, we're all sinners! I already know that!"

I said patiently, "Dad, just say it."

He repeated it out loud. I continued, "I believe you died for my sins."

"Of course, he died for our sins! Everybody knows that!"

"Dad, just say it."

And on and on we went through the whole prayer, Dad arguing with me over every single line. When we went through the prayer and Dad said Amen, I looked up, and in my mind, I said to God, *I'll have to keep my mouth shut now. The rest is up to you.*

My dad was a military dad. He was harsh and direct. And what a penny pincher he was! I watched in awe as my dad softened visibly and so quickly after that Sunday. He started making jokes, and I realized my dad was downright funny. He could have been a stand-up comedian. He started being generous with his money. There was no doubt in my mind that as much as he had argued with me, he evidently meant it when he repeated that prayer with me.

You will know them by their fruits. Do men gather grapes from thorn bushes or figs from thistles? Even so, every good tree bears good fruit, but a bad tree bears bad fruit. A good tree cannot bear bad fruit, nor can a bad tree bear good fruit. Every tree that does not bear good fruit is cut down and thrown into the fire. Therefore by their fruits you will know them. (Matt. 7:16–20)

God's Amazing Love

Summer 1989

One lovely summer day, I was out hanging clothes. I was talking to God as I usually do whenever I can do some brainless activity that I don't have to concentrate on. I was just telling him how wonderful he is.

"God, you're so amazing. I can't believe you would spend a single ounce of energy on an idiot like me."

I was going on and on about his mercy and goodness and how he takes care of me and my family, when I felt an unexplainable joy begin to descend upon me. It was the most amazing feeling.

It had begun quite softly, but I felt it enough that I stopped in my tracks, in the middle of hanging one of Arty's T-shirts on the line. I stood there and just felt it. It began to grow, and I'm sorry that I just can't even describe it. I can't put into words what it felt like, but even now, I can remember it so vividly.

As I stood there, just enjoying God's caress, the feeling became so strong that it was overpowering me. I felt honestly like I was going to pass out.

I said, "Lord, I love you so much and I love feeling you love me, but please stop because I am going to faint!"

And so he did immediately, and I was so sorry I had asked him to stop.

> For I am persuaded that neither death nor life, nor angels nor principalities nor powers, nor things present nor things to come, nor height nor depth, nor any other created thing, shall be able to separate us from the love of God which is in Christ Jesus our Lord. (Rom. 8:38–39)

One Fateful Saturday

August 1989

My parents drove the kids to Minnesota to visit my uncle and his family. Adam was six years old and Alexis was four, almost five. Arty and I had some time on our hands so we went to watch a baseball game at the local high school. When we came home, we had a message from a nurse at St. Francis Hospital in the Twin Cities saying that Alexis had been bitten in the face by a dog, but she was okay. The nurse left a number for me to call.

When I called, Dad told me what had happened. My uncle was living in a house he had designed and had built into a hill. He had a three-year-old Great Dane named Duke. Oh, how Duke loved Alexis as he followed her everywhere. He would even sit outside the bathroom door, waiting for her.

My uncle, my parents, and the kids had gone to breakfast. When they came home, Alexis and Adam went running down the hill toward the corner of the house. Unbeknownst to them, Duke was running around the house toward the same corner to meet them. They collided, and Duke lashed out in fear. He bit Alexis twice before Adam was able to calm him down.

My uncle scooped Alexis up in his arms and ran her to the kitchen to clean her up and assess the injury. Alexis never cried or even whimpered. Uncle Bill saw her bite marks, and her nose flap barely hanging on. He covered her face with a wet washcloth and they rushed her to the hospital.

As they waited in the emergency room, Alexis looked at her grandpa. She said, "Oh, Grandpa, I got blood on your clean white shirt." My military dad just about lost it.

Then the doctor walked in to explain Duke had bit Alexis, tearing through the flap on her nose, barely leaving it intact at the top. He tore through her upper lip, and his next bite almost cut through the carotid artery in her neck. She was a very lucky girl. Minnesota's number one plastic surgeon was on call that weekend and would arrive in about twenty minutes.

Dad said, "Get on a plane right now. I will reimburse you for the ticket."

I hung up, frantically called the airline, and told them what had happened. The reservationist gave me a round-trip ticket at half price for a medical emergency. I packed my bag and we drove off for Stapleton Airport. Just after we left the house, I realized I was leaving Arty with no money and nothing to eat, so we stopped in at the ATM at Safeway to grab a couple hundred dollars for him.

We parked Arty's old pickup truck and ran into the airport to catch my flight. As we went up to the counter to pay for my ticket, I handed the agent my credit card. He came back to say that it had declined. I told him it was a brand new credit card, and I had never even used it. He said that it being a weekend, there was, unfortunately, no way to contact the credit card company to find out why it had been declined.

I began to break down. Arty explained what had happened. He asked how much the ticket was, and the agent said it came to $412. Arty said, "What if we just fly her one way?" The agent replied that it would then be $206. Arty offered the agent the $200 cash in his pocket, and the agent said he could not discount the ticket. The agent really was quite rude.

At that point, I lost it. I laid my head on my hand on the counter, began slapping the counter with my other hand, crying out, "Jesus, please help me! Please help me!" Arty began patting me on the back and saying, "Honey, you should calm down now," as he watched a security guard heading our way. Just then, the agent said, "All right. I'll go ahead and give you the ticket for $200." Arty gladly handed over the cash. As he did, he felt in his pocket and realized he only had a quarter left. Even back then, that was not enough to get his truck out of the parking lot. The agent replied, "Cleaned you out, did we? Gee, that's a shame."

As we sat down on a bench to wait for my flight, I was worried that Arty couldn't get out of the lot and had no money for groceries. He said, "Let's just get more money out." I told him that we had cleaned out our checking account for the cash. He said, "This is an emergency. Give me the ATM card and let's see if it will go through." I searched everywhere and could not find the card. As though matters could not get worse, I realized I had left it on the ATM machine at Safeway.

I began to cry again. As Arty was trying to comfort me, a lady sitting at the opposite end of the bench leaned over tentatively and asked, "Are you on vacation?" Arty and I laughed and said no and then we told her what had happened. She said, "Oh, my husband is in the restroom. We can help!" Her husband joined us, and after hearing the story, he handed us a twenty-dollar bill. I asked for their address so we could send them a check but they declined, instructing us to pass the blessing along.

So off I went to Minnesota, crying all the way and wondering who had my ATM card, how my poor husband was going to buy groceries, and worried sick to death about my miracle baby's second close call.

I arrived at the airport, and Dad was waiting at the gate. He escorted me quickly to his SUV. As he started the truck, I looked down at the trash can and saw my sweet daughter's pink and white-striped top lying there. I picked it up, and it was soaked in her blood. I began to cry again, and Dad snatched it out of my hand and told me I had to be strong for Alexis. I immediately dried my eyes and calmed down.

Dad explained on the way that she had been taken into surgery and it took fifty-eight stitches just to close up the tears in her face. Then he told me about my six-year-old Adam taking his savings down to the gift shop where he picked out a cross necklace for his little sister. He carefully poured out all his change. When the clerk had counted out the money, she leaned over and told Adam he was fifty cents short. Adam explained that his little sister had been bitten by a dog, and he really wanted to give her that necklace when she woke up. The clerk paid the fifty cents herself as tears welled up in her eyes. The blessings just kept coming for our family.

We walked for what seemed like an eternity before finally arriving at Alexis's bedside. As she turned toward me, I took in the swollen, stitch-covered face of my little angel. I asked her how she was doing, and she said she was fine.

The surgeon then took me aside and explained it all to me. He felt everything had gone smoothly. His only concern was the bite through her upper lip. It had severed the nerves there, and he had done his best to sew them together. But he didn't know if she would ever be able to smile on that side of her face again. He said that later on we could take her in for scar revision.

Three days later, the IV started burning Alexis's little hand, and the nurse said she would have to move it to her other hand. She brought a package of M&Ms and told Alexis if she would be brave, she would give her the M&Ms. Alexis was so brave going through it, but I could tell by her face that it hurt, and it was taking everything she had not to cry. It was so hard watching her suffer that the tears started welling up in my eyes. After the nurse was done, Alexis noticed I was struggling and she said, "Mommy, if you stop crying, I'll give you an M&M."

Twenty-six years later, you can hardly see the scars now. She has a beautiful smile, and she still loves big black dogs.

> For I am the Lord who heals you. (Exod. 15:26)

Cold Turkey

November 1989

One day, Arty and I were reminiscing about the kids and talking about how fast they were growing up. Arty said, "Before you know it, Megan will be graduating." Megan was eight. I quickly replied back, "As much as you smoke, you won't be alive to see it!"

Later that afternoon, Megan came to me and said, "I wish my daddy would stop smoking." I suggested we pray about it, and so we did.

That evening, I received a phone call from my friend Sue. She was entering a program at Kaiser to help people quit smoking and was required to bring along an accountability partner. She asked for my permission to speak with Arty about it. I said, "Of course, that would be great!"

Sue and Arty started the program and quit smoking the next week. Arty hasn't had a cigarette in over twenty-five years!

> Or do you not know that your body is the temple of the Holy Spirit who is in you, whom you have from God, and you are not your own? For you were bought at a price; therefore glorify God in your body and in your spirit, which are God's. (1 Cor. 6:19–20)

That Was Stupid

Summer 1990

I was doing my weekly shopping at the grocery store, going up and down the aisles, when I passed by a family going the opposite direction. There was a dad, mom, and three small children. As I passed by, the man was loudly rebuking his wife and yelling at his children. The mom looked embarrassed and scared. I thought to myself, *How horrible.* I wondered, *If this man is acting like this in public, what might be happening inside their home?* I cried out in my spirit to God and said, *Someone needs to witness to this man!*

As I traveled through the grocery store, going up and down the aisles, this family was going the same direction, so it forced me to view the embarrassing spectacle over and over again. I asked the Lord again, *Send someone to witness to this family!*

After a few more trips up and down the aisles, it finally dawned on me the Lord was sending someone, and it was me! I then thought, *Oh, no! He's big and scary! I don't want anything to do with him! I wouldn't know what to say! How am I going to witness to someone in the middle of the grocery store?* Besides, I was almost finished shopping and ready to check out.

I pushed my cart to the shortest line and waited. I could see the family at the ice cream freezer and the dad still going on. I felt guilty, knowing the Lord wanted me to do something, but still too scared to even think straight. I prayed silently, *Lord, if you want me to say anything to that man, you will have to get them to come directly over here to my line right now.*

I watched them out of the corner of my eye in shock as they immediately stopped what they were doing and guided their cart and the children straight over to my line and stopped behind me. I was so scared as they stood behind me, and he continued to nag at his wife. As I was checking out, I frantically tried to think of what I could say. As the checker handed me my receipt, I turned around and the words burst from my mouth, "You need Jesus!" and I ran my cart away from them as fast as I could!

I got into my car and just shook my head. Why is it I am so afraid to tell people of the love and mercy they can find in Jesus? It should be the easiest message to share.

> For God has not given us a spirit of fear, but of power and of love and of a sound mind. Therefore do not be ashamed of the testimony of our Lord... (2 Tim. 1:7–8)

Special Forces Angel

Spring 1991

Being in a blended family is not easy. When the ex-wife gets involved, issues multiply even more. What seemed like no problem became inflated mountains of drama every week. After four years of trying to survive her constant haranguing and her scheming to make me out the villain, I was feeling beaten down and totally intimidated. My daily prayer was for deliverance.

We were still attending Faith at this time, and there was a mother-daughter banquet coming up. I wanted to take Alexis and Megan to the dinner. A few days after I told Megan, she approached me about inviting her mom. I, of course, agreed with trepidation. If I said no, her mother would just use it to place another nail in my coffin. So the plans were made, and I spent the next couple of weeks trying to survive anxiety attacks.

A couple of weeks prior, I was leaving the church one Sunday when I noticed a beautiful woman sitting alone in the pew. I was unexplainably drawn to her and introduced myself. Her name was Lynn, and we immediately became friends.

A few days before the banquet, I thought about inviting Lynn for moral support and as a distraction from the oppressive presence of the ex. Lynn gladly accepted, and I immediately felt relief and was able to breathe again.

The dinner went well. Megan's mother got some extra time with Megan, and Lynn and I enjoyed time with Alexis. At the end of the dinner, Lynn took me aside and told me she didn't know why I allowed Megan's mother to dominate me or to make me feel inadequate in any way. She said, "Linda, she can't hold a candle to you."

I treasured Lynn's encouragement and support, especially since she totally disappeared out of my life after that night.

> I have called upon You, for You will hear me, O God; incline Your ear to me, and hear my speech. Show Your marvelous lovingkindness by Your right hand, O You who save those who trust in You from those who rise up against them. (Ps. 17:6–7)

It's Not the TV

Summer 1997

Alexis has always had trouble sleeping. She found out that she could go to sleep easier if she was watching television in her room. She kept her door closed since her room was on the garden level and everyone kept her awake otherwise. I was in the habit of going to her door and praying for her at night before I would retire to my own bed. As I went to her door one night, however, I could hear a gravelly voice that made my hair stand up on the back of my neck. It was speaking in a language I could not understand.

As I fought back the fear, I thought maybe she fell asleep and had left her television on, and I was hearing a movie or something. I tentatively opened the door and stared into the pitch-black darkness of her room. There was not a sound, and her television was not on.

The next morning, after Arty left for work and the kids were in school, I went to work. I went down to Alexis's room and began to pray, asking God what I should do. God did not speak to me as much as I could sense his instruction. It became clear very quickly that I was to get some olive oil and anoint all the windows and doors with it—rebuking, binding, and casting out the demon in the name of Jesus. I asked God, "Well, do I just use plain old olive oil?" He then instructed me to pray over it first, of course.

I performed the anointing throughout the house as I was told. I never encountered that demon again.

> And as he was still coming, the demon threw him down and convulsed him. Then Jesus rebuked the unclean spirit, healed the child, and gave him back to his father. (Luke 9:42–43)

Tithe? Are You Crazy?

December 1999

Arty bugged me about tithing for several years while the kids were young. I always replied, "Are you crazy? We can't even afford shoelaces for the kids, and you want to give ten percent to the church?"

After a few years of guilt trips down the road of sermons, self-analyzation, and Bible studies ad nauseam, I was listening to a pastor teaching on the radio who said, "If you are having financial difficulties, it is because you aren't tithing."

Wow! I started thinking on a totally different track. All of a sudden, what the Scriptures say about giving took on a whole new light. It was December of 1999. For the first time in twelve years of marriage, we had saved up $1,000 in our savings account, and Arty had received a $1,500 bonus just before Christmas for the past seven years. We decided to try tithing. If it didn't work, we had backup!

That Sunday, I wrote our first check to the church. On Wednesday, the radiator went out in our station wagon. Repair was $500. That's okay. We still had $500 in savings.

I wrote another check to the church that next Sunday. On Tuesday, the compressor broke in our refrigerator.

Repair was another $500. That's okay. We're still getting that bonus check next week.

Then I wrote a check to the church the next Sunday after that and waited for Arty's bonus check. But no bonus came that year.

That's when I started asking God what went wrong. I realized we were either being tempted by the devil or being tested by God. Either way, we had no choice but to continue tithing. I finally understood I had tried to tithe on my own steam. I thought I had it all figured out.

That is when I turned our finances over to the Lord. We decided 10 percent of every paycheck, tax refund, rebate, or any kind of income was going to the church along with a prayer that God would handle our finances from that point forward.

I'm not saying it's always easy to write that check to the church, but God has never let us down. After three months of tithing faithfully, I realized I had not had to put groceries back after the bill was rung up, and our bills were being paid on time with a little left over for savings or maybe even a dinner out.

When our finances are strapped, I don't think twice about writing that check because it's not about the money. It's about Jesus!

> So let each one give as he purposes in his heart, not grudgingly or of necessity, for God loves a cheerful giver. (2 Cor. 9:7)

Do You Need a Job?

January 2002

I had been working at my favorite chiropractor's office for quite some time and was struggling through it every day. Being a secretary/bookkeeper—and at that time, not confident in my abilities as a chiropractic assistant—I was coming to the end of my rope. I had tied a knot and was holding on for dear life.

Just as I was coming to the decision that I should do my chiropractor a favor and resign, 9/11 happened. I was so afraid I wouldn't be able to get work again. But a few days later, I came home in tears. Arty comforted me and told me to turn in my keys the next day. He said, "Just trust God. It will be fine."

So the next morning, I resigned with no notice. I just couldn't take it anymore. I began to put out my résumés. With my skills, I had not had any problem finding employment since high school. However, after submitting over two hundred applications and not even being called for an interview, it was looking pretty dismal.

Arty and I prayed. The church prayed. Our Christian friends prayed. Still nothing after three months.

We had been fairly active in the pro-life arena with Colorado Right to Life. I know more about abortion than I really want to know. I approached Arty about my theory that perhaps God wanted me to volunteer with Colorado Right to Life. I just knew the churches were the answer to turning around that heinous Roe v. Wade decision. I wanted to be a liaison between the churches and Colorado Right to Life to call the churches into action. Arty agreed.

I called Colorado Right to Life and spoke with Cleta. I was so excited about my idea, so I went on and on. She listened patiently and then said, "That would be wonderful, but you don't need a job, do you?"

I started the next Monday as Colorado Right to Life's state office manager.

> For You formed my inward parts; You covered me in my mother's womb, I will praise You, for I am fearfully and wonderfully made; Marvelous are Your works, and that my soul knows very well. My frame was not hidden from You, when I was made in secret, and skillfully wrought in the lowest parts of the earth. (Ps. 139:13–15)

Pepper

April 2002

Seven years ago, our little Basset Hound, Cleo, had to be put down. We were missing her company, so we visited our local Dumb Friends League. I was praying for a dog like my Gypsy that I had when I was eighteen years old. She was a black and white border collie. Unbeknownst to us, Lex was praying for a big black dog like the one that bit her!

My border collie was there, but so was a black lab/Rottweiler mix that Lex laid eyes on. Lex fell so in love with that dog, but we were second in line. Someone had beat her to the punch. Arty was adamant also that we were not getting two dogs. As we sat there, Lexy began to cry, and we tried to comfort her while Arty steamed. Just then a couple walked over to us—the man and his wife who had put in for Lexy's dog. She knelt down in front of Lex and said, "I wanted that dog so much until I found out that you were here for her too. I think she would rather be with a child who can play with her. We will find another dog."

Megan and Adam joined forces with Lex against their dad and somehow we ended up with two dogs. Lex paid for the black lab, so she was her dog, and Lex renamed her

Pepper. Arty was irritated as we loaded the dogs up in our station wagon. We intentionally put Pepper in the front seat beside Arty and watched her melt Arty's heart.

Fast forward to a Saturday in April 2002. The kids were away, and Arty and I were at home doing yard work and chores. Arty noticed Pepper in the backyard, wandering around, seeming with a purpose, looking behind bushes. Arty called her and couldn't get her attention. He instinctively knew she was looking for a place to lie down to die. He ran over to her and noticed she wasn't acting right, so he called to me, we bundled her up in the car, and drove her to the vet's office.

The vet checked her out and explained that being a large breed, she had a common problem where her intestines had twisted. It would take surgery soon or she would need to be put down. She was Lexy's dog, so we prayed that God would help us find her and make her answer her phone.

We put in the call, and Lex answered right away. She and Adam were just up the street having pizza. They came immediately, and Lex had a tough decision to make. Pepper didn't suffer long.

> A righteous man regards the life of his animal.
> (Prov. 12:10)

Fred

June 2004

After the divorce, I made sure my former parents-in-law were able to spend time with their grandchildren regularly, and we were still on good terms, so Arty and I would visit occasionally.

During one of our visits, Fred and Arty were standing in the driveway on a sunny summer day, and Arty spoke to Fred a little about the Lord and being born again. Fred's response was pretty much the same as my mom's. He said he guessed he was going to hell then.

Some time later, Fred was diagnosed with a brain tumor. His decline was fairly rapid, and a few months later, he was confined to a wheelchair, unable to speak and having a hard time hearing. He was in a nursing home and my parents and I had driven out to visit with him.

As we sat in the room, I began to pray for Fred's salvation. All of a sudden, the Lord said, "Ask him again." So I knelt by Fred's wheelchair and said, "Fred, do you remember Arty talking to you about being born again?" Fred grunted and nodded his head slightly. I asked if he would like to say the prayer, and again, he grunted and nodded his head. I asked him to simply repeat the prayer silently as Mom, Dad, and I rejoiced with him and the angels in heaven.

Shortly thereafter, Fred was moved to hospice and had fallen into a coma. One night, I returned home after work to get ready for a class at church when I became agitated in my spirit and told Arty I had to go out to the hospice to be with Fred.

I arrived to find Fred alone so I pulled up a chair and began to speak with him, singing Jesus songs and reading scriptures to him. Sometime in the wee hours of the night, one of Fred's eyes popped open. I panicked and ran to get someone. The nurses came in, and they checked Fred's vitals and turned him. They told me I should call Fran. A few minutes later, Fred passed away.

> What man of you, having a hundred sheep, if he loses one of them, does not leave the ninety-nine in the wilderness and go after the one which is lost until he finds it? And when he has found it, he lays it on his shoulders, rejoicing. And when he comes home, he calls together his friends and neighbors, saying to them, 'Rejoice with me, for I have found my sheep which was lost!' I say to you that likewise there will be more joy in heaven over one sinner who repents than over ninety-nine just persons who need no repentance. (Luke 15:4–7)

Mom's Homecoming

July 2004

My dad called me at work on July 26 to tell me that Mom was in the hospital for some tests. He explained he had found Mom that morning on the floor, unable to get to the bathroom. She was picked up by ambulance and rushed to the hospital. I called Arty, who immediately told me to get down there.

When I arrived, it was as though she didn't recognize me. She was fighting to get out of the bed while being hooked up to an IV and catheter. I was physically trying to keep her in bed when the ER doctor arrived. Watching me for some time wrestle with my mom, as he sat patiently and not even offering any assistance, he asked, "Is she normally like this?"

It turned out that because the only problem Mom had ever had to go to the hospital for was related to her upper GI, that was all they were looking for. Seven hours later, they finally did a spinal tap and found blood. They immediately realized that she had an aneurysm that had burst in her brain. We had no idea when it had happened, but she may have had blood surging into her brain for possibly sixteen hours. They flew her to St. Joseph's Hospital and performed surgery the next morning. She came out of the surgery completely comatose and on life support.

Mom had never liked doctors, and I knew she would not like this situation. She hated it, but Dad had been a believer in doctors all his life. How could I convince him to take Mom off life support and let her go? I couldn't. I just had to keep my peace and let it play out.

Wednesday morning, I woke up agitated, pacing the floor, and crying out to God. I found myself repeating, "This isn't right. This isn't what Mom would want!" Then the phone rang. It was Dad, sobbing. He said, "Linda, please come to the hospital. I need you." I asked him what was wrong, and he said he would tell me when I got there.

When I arrived, Dad explained that he woke up in the middle of the night and immediately went to his knees beside his bed to pray. Then a bright light lit up the bedroom, and he heard a voice say, "Elmer, this isn't what Gloria would want."

Then he said to me, "Linda, we need to take her off life support."

I said, "Okay, Dad."

When the doctor arrived, he said we were taking away any chance she had to survive. I asked him, then, what exactly is her chance? He explained she had definitely lost her ability to control her tongue because she had a device in her mouth to keep her from swallowing it. She had possibly a twenty percent chance of living a somewhat normal life after maybe a year of rehabilitation. She could wake up blind and/or unable to speak. I told him that didn't sound very promising to me, and add to that her living will that stated she did not want to be on life support longer than seventy-two hours. We told him about Dad's vision. The doctor agreed reluctantly to remove the life support the next morning.

I began to make calls to notify relatives. When I returned to the room, I was holding Mom's hand and telling Dad that I had spoken with their nephew, Bob, who was residing in Arizona. He said he could not get a flight until the next day and so would be there by Friday. All of a sudden, Mom gripped my hand hard, tensing up so much that her blood pressure alarm went off! I turned to her and said, "Okay, Mom, but you're going to have to hang around until Friday if you want to see Bobby."

After everything was removed from Mom and she was resting peacefully, I went to speak with two of the nurses at their station and told them I was concerned that Mom was still here. The nurses explained that she could linger. I was afraid perhaps that we had made the wrong decision. The nurses both reassured me and said that Mom was lucky to have us and that it was for the best. That night, Mom's breathing became noticeably more labored. I was spending the nights with Mom in her room on a recliner that kept folding up on me. I guess it would have been pretty comical except for the seriousness of the situation.

By Friday, both of my cousins, Bob and Bill, were there with Mom and Dad, Arty and me. We were talking and having a great time when I suddenly noticed that Mom had grown very still, and I could not hear her breathing. I quietly walked over to her and put my ear to her face so I could feel her breath. Then I realized she was trying to hear every word. I smiled and sat back down to let her enjoy the evening.

After everyone left, I settled into the recliner to spend the night again and noticed that Mom's breathing had become even more labored. By Saturday morning, she was really struggling. I was getting more concerned so I asked the nurse standing by her bed. She explained that in the old days, before all the technology that artificially keeps people alive, this is how they passed on. Eventually, she just wouldn't be able to breathe anymore.

The nurse was so beautiful. She had long blonde hair in a braid down her back. She stayed with me and Mom. I turned to Mom and said, "Mom, you know Jesus. You know where you're going. You have nothing to be afraid of. We'll all see you later. Why don't you pack your bags, board the Glory Train, and go home?" Arty and Dad walked in then. I waited while she labored for air for a minute and turned to the nurse and said, 'You know, she never listens to me." The nurse smiled. About thirty seconds later, Mom's breathing became quiet and peaceful and then she was gone.

A little while later, the doctor stopped by and quietly confided in me that he felt we were right and it was a good decision. I was so relieved and I thanked him.

A few days later, I approached Dad. All the nurses who had taken care of Mom had been so wonderful. I asked Dad if he would help me present them with a little paperweight gift. He said he would like that. I called the hospital and the head nurse looked in Mom's file to get the names of all her nurses. I told her I would drop the gifts off after having them made. She said the nurses have a meeting every week, and she would like us to present them at the meeting. She explained that would be an encouragement to all the nurses there. I agreed. I had the awards made up. They were crystal paperweights with a flat globe imprinted in the background. Inscribed on them were the nurses' individual names, Mom's name, her dates of birth and death, and the statement "You made a world of difference."

Dad and I went to the meeting. He said he wasn't up to it and asked if I could present the awards. He took his seat, and I presented the awards to each one of the nurses, sharing individual special memories, until they introduced the nurse who had taken care of Mom the day she passed away. I stared in disbelief as I handed her the award. My dad and I had never seen her before!

Could it be that the beautiful nurse by Mom's bedside when she died was an angel sent by God to take her home?

> Be not forgetful to entertain strangers; for thereby some have entertained angels unawares. (Heb. 13:2)

Heinz

September 2004

After mom caught the Glory Train, Dad told me how she had begged him to go to church with her and that he had refused. He felt horrible guilt, and I told him I thought Mom would like it if he went now. Better late than never.

Dad had really connected with the ladies of Mom's Presbyterian church when they had provided the meal after her memorial service. He thought they were wonderful. I said, "Why don't you go visit a few times?" He was bent on going to the local Lutheran church. I wondered why he would rather go to a church where no one knew him. "At least," I coaxed, "at Mom's church, you would have a connection there through her." But he was adamant that he was going to visit the Lutheran church.

I asked the Lord to nudge Dad over to Mom's church. Dad spoke fluent German and was always talking to us in German. We loved listening to him and would beg him not to stop. I thought how cool would it be if there was someone at Mom's church who could speak German with Dad. I asked God if he could have someone there.

A few days later, Dad told me he thought he would stop by Mom's church the next Sunday. I told him I was thrilled as I smiled to myself and thanked God for his promptings.

The next Sunday afternoon, Dad called me. He said he had visited Mom's church. He told me as he had approached the front door, the greeter held out his hand to welcome Dad. He said, "Welcome brother, I'm Heinz." Dad recognized the German name and replied in German that it was nice to meet him. Heinz replied back in German. It was to be the beginning of a wonderful friendship. Heinz invited Dad to his weekly Bible study. Dad never missed a Sunday meeting or Bible study until he went home to be with the Lord.

Dad used to pick up two or three extra bags of groceries every week to drop them off at the church office, reminding Carol, "Now who brought these?" Carol would reply, "I believe it was Mr. Anonymous." Dad would nod and be on his way.

Auf wiedersehen.

> Casting all your care upon Him, for He cares for you. (1 Pet. 5:7)

Dad's Homecoming

September 2006

Dad was my rock. Whenever I ran into trouble, I turned to him, whether it was financial difficulties or just the need for counseling or someone to talk to. He had osteoarthritis in his back and a heart condition. He had just endured back surgery that had put him in more pain than he was in before the procedure. After Mom died, he was so depressed and lonely. I worried constantly about him dying alone. I prayed, asking God to please have someone there with him when it was his time to go.

Dad always said that he had fixed it with "the man upstairs" and was going to have a heart attack and go quickly.

We were also so proud at this time that Adam was graduating from college that December. Dad was paying for a large portion of Adam's school, and he would be the first to graduate college in Dad's line.

The second week of September, Dad's sister, Norma, came out to visit for a couple of weeks. One early morning, just before Norma was to return home, Dad knocked on her door and said that he was having chest pains and should probably go to the hospital. Aunt Norma drove Dad to the hospital and he had that massive heart attack exactly the way he wanted it to go.

The doctor told me the first thing Dad had said to him was that he thought it would be a good day to see Jesus. The doctor said anytime he hears that, he figures it's pretty much over.

A few days later Adam said he understood my prayer and that Aunt Norma was there to take Grandpa to the hospital, but he didn't understand why God honored my prayer for Grandpa and took him before he could see Adam graduate. I replied, "Are you kidding? Of course he was there and he had the best seat in the house!"

> Your eyes saw my substance, being yet unformed. And in Your book they all were written. The days fashioned for me, when as yet there were none of them. (Ps. 139:16)

Lady

October 2006

We brought Lady home from the Dumb Friend's League eleven years ago. She was a border collie and was the dopiest dog we've ever had. But she and I fell in love with each other at first sight. When the handler walked her into the room to get to know us a little, she ignored everyone else and walked up to me, stood up on her back legs to place her front legs on my shoulders, and gave me a little doggie kiss right off the bat. It was over then and there, and she was mine and I was hers.

As soon as we got her home, we knew we were in trouble. She liked to eat the toilet paper off the rolls, so we had to immediately move all the toilet paper to where she couldn't reach it. She also decided it was important to urinate all over the beds as soon as we left her. So the bedroom doors had to remain shut at all times since she eventually decided we didn't have to be gone for her to mark her territory. Then she decided since the beds were no longer available, she would mark the couches! We then had to keep the couches covered. But oh, how she grinned when we walked in the door.

She was very protective of me. Arty and I would lounge on the couch watching TV. She would jump up on my lap, flatten herself out over me, and growl and snap at Arty. He would grab her playfully by the scruff of her neck and her backside and toss her off onto the floor. Before her feet were even under her, she would scramble back up to the same position and begin to growl at him again. The Dumb Friend's League advised us to immediately bring her back because they said her behavior would accelerate and she would eventually bite. But she never did, and we just couldn't give her up anyway.

One day I was carrying a load of laundry downstairs, again talking to God since laundry is fairly brainless work. I asked him why he loved us. We are so stupid and weak and selfish. I just couldn't understand why he even bothers with us. At that moment, I looked to my left and there was Lady sitting there under the kitchen table.

> I am the good shepherd. The good shepherd gives His life for the sheep…I am the good shepherd; and I know My sheep, and am known by My own. As the Father knows me, even so I know the Father; and I lay down my life for the sheep. (John 10:11, 14–15)

Saving the Gym

December 2007

When Alexis was five, she started taking gymnastics. When she was thirteen, she was a Level 10 gymnast, and she came home announcing that she was going to own a gymnastics school. I said, "That's nice, honey."

After she graduated high school and tried a couple of other jobs, Alexis found an ad for a head coach/office manager at Castle Rock School of Gymnastics and called about the job. Her old trainer answered the phone. When she told him who she was, he said, "Lexy! Come in Monday! You're hired!"

After working there three years, the owners offered her the gym. She was so excited when she called me, but I had to remind her that neither she nor her dad or I had any money.

Arty and I had just paid off our house, and he was working out of town in Springerville, Arizona. When he called that night, I asked if we could put another mortgage on our home to help Lex get the gym. There was dead silence at the other end of the line.

After discussing it and praying about it, we decided to ask a friend of ours who co-owned the Cummins dealership to take a look at the numbers for us and tell us if he thought it would be too risky or not. We waited on his answer, praying all the while that he would say no. We were scared spitless. We told Lex that if Joe came back with a yes, we would do it for her. But if he said no, we would not.

The fateful day arrived and Joe said we should give it a shot. Arty and I both said, "Oh no!" But we decided we would step out in faith and that it was God's answer to our prayers, and we should not second-guess God. I gave notice at Colorado Right to Life, and Lex and I signed the papers and bought a gymnastics school. I had told Lex earlier that I would be working with her.

She said, "Yes, Mother."

I said, "I will be paying the bills."

"Yes, Mother."

"I will pay our house payment first!"

"Yes, Mother."

Lex didn't tell me until after the papers were signed, "Oh, by the way, we need to save up $35,000 by May because enrollment drops in the summer." Well, thanks for the warning.

Two weeks later, Dad went home to be with the Lord. Being the only kid, it fell to me to clean up his affairs and settle his estate. It was just as the housing bubble was collapsing, so I had a serious undertaking on my hands. Dad's house in

Thornton was a half hour north of my home in Aurora, and the gym was a little over a half hour south, giving me what could have been an impossible task of keeping up with both homes and the gym, especially with Arty out of town. I will be eternally grateful to Dad's friends from his church, Rob and his dad, who did all the shoveling and maintenance for Dad's home in Thornton until I could sell it.

Add all of this to just starting a new business and being scared out of my mind, I was pretty much a wreck.

Christmas eve, our church moved out of the school where we were meeting and moved into their new building. We had a dove on the pulpit but no cross, and Pastor Ed started talking about plans for a cross between the screens up front. It was very important to me to have a cross.

That January was the month when we were snowed in three weekends in a row. Our business lost a lot of income. In May, enrollment started to drop just as Lex had predicted, but we only had $18,000 saved. Then in June, Arty had to have open heart surgery and was off work for five months.

By November, my dog died, I had put in another $18,000 of my inheritance, and we still only had half of our $15,000 rent payment. I asked Pastor Ed about that scripture that says God won't give us more than we can handle. He said it goes more like God will give you whatever it takes to break you so you will let him take over. I was going to find out soon how that felt.

I told Lex about our financial situation. She was stressed out and afraid we would lose the house. We called our landlord, but he said not to worry about it, just to pay what we could for now. I sent him $7,500 and began to worry about the next month.

By December, we had collected most of our tuition and still had only $12,000 in the bank, and rent was due the next week. That morning found me lying in a puddle at the foot of my stairs, sobbing and crying out to God. I raised my hand up and said, "The gym is yours, Lord. I can't do this anymore. Put us in a cardboard box. I don't care anymore. Just please, you have to tell me what to do. Do I walk away or put more money in to try to save the gym? I don't know what to do!"

I cleaned up and drove in to the gym and told Lex about my prayer. She did the deposit and said, "Mom, we made $9,000. That's a pretty good deposit. What do you think?" I made the calculations, and we had a total of $21,000. Then I got the rent statement. The landlords had placed the remainder of the October rent on that statement with $22,500 owing for December and the statement in bold print "$750 Penalty Waived One Time Only." It then dawned on me that we had a $6,000 payroll that Friday. Lex asked, "Are we done?" I told her I felt like God was telling us to wait, so we did.

We still did not have a cross up at the church. Arty had returned to work after his surgery, but he was still running on fumes by the end of each workday. He came home that Wednesday night looking pretty worn out. I told him about my prayer that morning and what had transpired that day. I explained that I felt like God wanted us to go to church that night. Arty replied, "Let me get cleaned up!" He showered and we ate and headed off to Calvary.

We arrived about ten minutes late, so everyone was already in the service. It was dark inside the sanctuary. As we opened the door, there was the cross bathed in golden light. I knew God was telling me to just trust him.

I can't explain how it happened, but by the next week, we paid the rent and payroll and had $5,000 left over. Our enrollment increased over one hundred kids each of the next three months, and the next summer, we didn't even have to dig into our savings.

It was at this time that I realized all those years, my rock and my sanctuary were not in my earthly dad, but in my heavenly Father. He had been there all the while just waiting for me to finally come wholeheartedly to him.

> Trust in the Lord with all your heart, and do not lean on your own understanding. (Prov. 3:5)

> For I know the plans I have for you, declares the Lord, plans for peace and not of evil, to give you a future and a hope. (Jer. 29:11)

Calvary Chapel Pagosa Springs

Summer 2009

Even though Arty and I played only a small part in this wonderful story, I felt God would like it included in this book.

Pastor Andrew was serving as the youth pastor at Calvary Aurora. Pagosa was birthed in Pastor Andrew's heart during a hunting trip to Pagosa Springs in 2007. Pastor Andrew and his wife Ronda were in Pagosa Springs one weekend, and Andrew was saying how great it would be to have a Calvary Chapel there. A couple of days after his trip, one of the pastors at Calvary Aurora retrieved a voice mail from an individual inquiring about the possibility of sending a pastor to plant a Calvary Chapel in Pagosa Springs! It was obvious who the message was for.

For two years, Andrew and Ronda prayed over Pagosa. The calling to plant Calvary Pagosa became evident during the summer of 2009. Their house was on the market, and they were planning to start a home inspection business anyway. The Lord spoke to them that if they were faithful to dwell in the land, he would provide for their needs.

When Arty and I heard that Andrew was planning to make a two-week trip to Pagosa Springs to check things out, we offered our twenty-four-foot travel trailer to him, not even knowing of their prayers or their needs. It was just sitting empty with no one using it anyway, which was unusual since Arty had been out of town for the previous three years. And even more amazing, Arty was not called out of town again until the Bakers no longer needed the trailer.

The Lord provided the way for Pastor Andrew and his family to relocate from Aurora, Colorado, to Pagosa Springs in October of 2009. Calvary Pagosa Springs services started the first Sunday in October 2009 in the Baker home and at the Pagosa Springs Youth Center the following Sunday.

> Trust in the Lord, and do good, dwell in the land, and feed on His faithfulness. (Psalm 37:3)

Be Careful What You Pray For

October 2010

Being in construction, Arty got laid off a lot up until he went out of town. He had been out of town off and on—more on than off—since Springerville in 2006, and I was getting tired of it. With his open heart surgery and the struggle of putting medications together, now having a trailer for him to live in, extra expenses that weren't reimbursed by the company, and just flat out missing him, I had had enough. He had been out of town again now for over a year, and it seemed like they just kept sending him farther and farther away. I was ready for him to come home for awhile. So that's what I prayed. "Lord, please, please, please send Arty home! I need him to be home for a while!"

Arty got his pink slip two days later. I told God that wasn't really what I had in mind. I could see God sitting there telling me, "You need to be more specific."

> Ask, and it will be given to you; seek, and you will find; knock, and it will be opened to you. For everyone who asks receives, and he who seeks finds, and to him who knocks it will be opened. (Matt. 7:7–8)

Jean

December 2010

Back when Arty and I decided that Faith Presbyterian Church would be our home—we found we were driving to Aurora three times a week—we made the decision to move, and I began praying for the perfect job again.

My first interview was at an insurance company. I met Jean, my soon-to-be new boss. As I sat in her office, I looked around at her Christian books and pictures and asked her if she was a Christian. She said she was. I asked, "Are you born again?" She replied, "Is there any other kind?" We laughed, and I replied, "I guess not."

In December of 1989, I was hired on the spot and there began our wonderful friendship. Jean was the one person who took a personal interest in me. Every morning, as I would start listening to a tape to get ready to transcribe her correspondence for her, Jean would begin with an encouraging word for me. She was so loving and kind. I had never before experienced such unconditional love in the workplace.

> A new commandment I give to you, that you love one another; as I have loved you; that you also love one another. By this all will know that you are My disciples, if you have love for one another. (John 13:34–35)

But all good things must come to an end. My children were six and eight years old. After three years and going through two caregivers, I wasn't willing to submit them once again to a babysitter and decided I was going to be a full-time mom. That night, I called Arty, who was now working on a construction project in Pueblo. I told him of my plans to quit working. He was aghast and asked how we would financially survive. I told him we would just trust God. He agreed reluctantly, so I gave notice to Jean the next morning.

That night, I received a call from my dad. He said he and my mom had decided that because they weren't able to give me a lot growing up, they wanted me to enjoy my inheritance now while they were still alive to see. They wanted to supplement Arty's income to help me stay at home with the kids. The best part is that I had not told them yet of my intentions.

Twenty years later, the kids were grown, and I started thinking back to Jean and her kindness and encouragement toward me. I really missed her, and I desperately wanted to get back in touch with her. I tried to look up the insurance company where we worked together, but it had since closed. I could not find her in the phone book anywhere in the

Denver metro area. I was at the end of my rope and cried out to God to help me find her somehow, some way.

A few days later, Arty was watching the news and I was puttering around the house as usual doing chores and catching up with administrative duties. I usually am so busy I don't even look up at the television when I'm passing by, but for some reason a story on the news caught my attention as I happened to be passing by and I saw Jean on the news! A thrift store in Longmont had been robbed just before Christmas and the reporter was putting out a call for anyone who wanted to donate to help them out.

We were able to hook up with Jean shortly thereafter and spent a wonderful afternoon with my old friend.

> There is a friend who sticks closer than a brother. (Prov. 18:24)

Anonymous Angel

December 2011

Even working out of town, Arty was still being laid off fairly regularly. A good friend had told me of a time when her husband had been out of work for a while. She had decided she would live on faith and not change anything financially. They did just fine, and God had come through in the end. I told Arty about it, and we decided we would try doing that, too.

The opportunity presented itself soon after. The year prior, Arty was laid off, and we had attended our favorite melodrama at Christmas with our friends at the gym. They had announced their New Year's Eve play and dance, and Arty and I decided then we would do that the next year. But that year, we were laid off again at Christmastime. Again, we attended our favorite play, and here they were, announcing the New Year's Eve dance. I reminded Arty of our friend's challenge and asked him if we shouldn't just step out in faith and go to that play and dance at New Year's Eve. We were tithing as usual but weren't sure if we should include those extravagant little extras. We asked God if it would be okay, and we decided to go for it—we purchased the tickets. We did the math and figured it would take $300 to attend the dance, stay in a motel that night, and have breakfast out the next morning.

New Year's Eve arrived and we set off for the play. We had enjoyed ourselves immensely and then decided we'd rather just go straight home. As we drove up, we noticed something taped on our door, and I retrieved it on the way in. It was an unsigned Christmas card with a $300 gift card inside. Guess we should have stayed overnight after all!

> But when you do a charitable deed, do not let your left hand know what your right hand is doing that your charitable deed may be in secret; and your Father who sees in secret will Himself reward you openly. (Matt. 6:6)

How Will People Know?

April 2013

After six years of searching, I finally found a great church again after leaving Faith. I love my church. I love my God. How can I get the word out to people so they can find what I have? I decided I would place business cards from Calvary Chapel, along with tracts on how to be saved, on the doors of homes around the church.

The first thing I needed to do was to find some kind of street map that would actually show the houses so I could mark them off and not double dip. After calling several businesses I thought might be able to provide a good map and checking everywhere on the Internet, I was at a dead-end.

Gee, maybe I should pray about it. "Well, Lord, I really could use a map. Could you help me find one?" Maybe I'll check the Internet again. Hmmm. There's one I didn't see before. I opened it up and it was a map of the entire city with grids and street names I could actually read. But I only need maybe a radius of six miles or so around the church. Well, maybe I could print the whole map out and use the copier at the gym to enlarge just the area around the church.

I clicked on the print button and a map came out of my printer on one 8½ by 11 sheet. Hmmm. It sure doesn't look like the whole city. Well, there's Hampden and there's Tower. Wow. There's Calvary smack dab in the center and all the neighborhoods within about six miles! Perfect.

> How then shall they call on Him in whom they have not believed? And how shall they believe in Him of whom they have not heard? And how shall they hear without a preacher? And how shall they preach unless they are sent? (Rom. 10:14–15)

My Demon

December 2013

While Adam was staying with us and Arty was popping in and out while being sent to the ends of the earth on construction projects, I had a most enlightening encounter. It started when Adam had a nightmare, and he told me about it the next morning.

He had been running for his life from something chasing him. Then he had tripped and fell down as the "monster" caught up to him. He could feel its hot breath on the back of his neck as he started to wake up from his dream. He turned his head to look up in the predawn gloom and saw something melt into the tie rack hanging on the back of his door.

After Adam left the house, I went into his room and felt the hairs stand up on the back of my neck and decided it was time to do some binding and casting in the name of Jesus. I went through the house and thought I had cleared it. Adam came home that night and asked, "Mom, you didn't get rid of anything in my room, did you? I really wanted to see if it would return tonight." I said, "Sorry, son, too late."

What I didn't know was that "that something" evidently decided it would rather torment me.

A few weeks later, Arty made it home. Unfortunately for me (in many ways), Arty can snore at such a decibel that he can literally rattle the windows throughout our modest home. I had learned many years prior that staying in the same room with him is not conducive to a restful sleep for me. But this was one of many nights that his snoring protection would have been welcomed.

I awakened for my normal visit to the bathroom around 2:00 a.m. I returned to my room, closed the door, and had just settled in when, all of a sudden, my bedroom light came on and then turned off again. I jumped from my bed asking, "Who did that? Who turned my light on?" I turned on the light and immediately noticed that the switch was silent. But earlier, the switch had made a quite audible clicking noise as it turned on and off. I looked around and no one was there.

I burst out into the hallway, but my son's bedroom door was closed and there wasn't a sound. I went into Arty's room and exclaimed, "Did you turn on my light?" Poor Arty came out of a dead sleep to say of course he had not. I told him something was in my room, and I started to cry. He offered to come in with me. As I lay in his protective arms, I stared into the pitch black with my eyes darting everywhere. I told him I couldn't sleep and went down to the computer. Of course, praying was the farthest thing from my mind. After all the years of answered prayers, I would think it would be the first thing to do. I don't have any excuses except that in this lesson, I seemed to be an extremely slow learner.

Anyway, the first web site I thought to visit was Ghost Hunters International. It said that if lights turned on by themselves, you should first have the wiring checked out in your house. If it was not faulty wiring, and it happened again, you should ask it to do it again.

Right, like that's gonna happen.

Arty left for Laredo, and I spent the next few nights in trepidation but had no interruptions. I convinced myself that it had been nothing. Just a fluke. I got comfortable sleeping by myself again, after having the wiring checked out, of course, and being told by a qualified electrician that everything was fine.

A few weeks later, while Arty was away from home, I got up for my usual visit to the bathroom and returned to bed. I was just settled in when something bumped against my bed, right by my left shoulder. I thought, perhaps, I wasn't as settled in as I thought and had moved the bed myself. Remembering what I had read previously, I quieted myself down and laid as still as possible before I asked, "Could you do that again?" It was quite compliant, and it immediately bumped my bed again at exactly the same place.

Strangely enough, I didn't get scared. I got mad. I have suffered from a severe sleep disorder since I was a child. I have had enough problems sleeping without some stupid ghost playing games with me. I proceeded to give it a good talking to, explaining that I didn't know what its deal was, but that I didn't care if it was in my room. Just leave me alone and let me sleep. I promptly turned over and was able to fall asleep again. (Of course, now I had discovered sleeping pills that were doing a great job as long as I wasn't interrupted too many times.)

I began to notice that I could feel the hairs on the back of my neck rise whenever I would enter my room to sleep at night. I pushed it off to my imagination and tried to ignore it most of the time.

Some time later, while Arty was again away, I woke up. I should tell you first though that being a creature of habit, I always go through my door without closing it, visit the bathroom, come back and shut my door to climb into bed. This time, however, my unwelcome friend had other ideas. As I came back to my room in the dark, I put out my hand to feel my way through the doorway and came into contact with my closed door. I thought, *That's weird*. I turned the knob to push open my door and could not open it. It felt as though someone, or something, was on the other side holding it closed. As I pushed harder, it let go all of a sudden and my door slammed open. I thought, *This thing doesn't want me in my own room!* I exclaimed, "Oh no you don't! I was here first! You're not scaring me out of my own room!" I promptly went to bed and went to sleep (after a quick prayer for protection). Thank God for sleeping pills.

At this point, I spoke with an herbalist friend of mine. She told me what to do. I promptly got some sage, lit it, and "smudged" the whole house, repeating, "Go to the light. You're not welcome here. You need to follow the light." Now I just shake my head thinking about it. It would have been pretty funny watching me do that.

As I went to church the next Sunday, I ran into Pastor Louie and told him what had been occurring in my room. I asked him if he believed in ghosts. He proceeded to explain that, according to the Bible, there is no such thing. It's pretty plain in God's Word that when you die, you either go to heaven or the other place. You don't hang around here. He said it's more likely an angel. Now you have to decide, is it a good or a bad angel? Well, I don't think a good angel would disturb my sleep or play games with me.

That means a demon. Oh dear! Now I was scared. I can handle a ghost. Not…well, that is a whole different thing.

I went home, prayed, and went through every room casting out the demon in the name of Jesus and anointing all my windows and doors with olive oil, after praying over it, of course.

A couple of months went by and everything seemed okay. The lull before the storm.

Since Adam had left home to start a career in firefighting in Charlotte, I was truly alone now. This time, I was awakened out of a deep slumber by something shaking my bed violently. As I woke up suddenly, the shaking stopped, and I felt something rise away from the crook of my elbow. Now I was scared. I knew what I was dealing with, but why didn't the casting and oil work this time?

I immediately dropped to my knees and begged God to tell me what to do. And then I knew. I found the scripture in my chronological Bible, Mark 5:1–9. I placed the Bible in the center of my headboard. That night, I felt completely at peace as I went to bed.

A couple of weekends later, Arty and I tried to sleep together, and then he left again for Laredo. That night, I felt that same eerie, hair tingling as I entered my room. I quickly looked at my Bible, but it looked different. It was opened to the Old Testament, and I could tell right away. I took it down, turned it back to Mark 5:1–9, and placed it back on my headboard. I called Arty and asked him if he might have accidentally flipped my Bible by hitting it in the middle of the night or something. He couldn't recall that happening, but of course, it was possible. At the same time, since he sleeps to the right of the Bible, it didn't make sense that he would flip it towards him to the Old Testament! I immediately got some Scotch tape, taped that Bible open to Mark 5:1–9. It hasn't budged since, and I have not been interrupted again.

If there is power in the Word to conquer demons, what might the Bible do for us if we actually read it?

> And they came to the other side of the sea, to the country of the Gadarenes.

And when He had come out of the boat, immediately there met Him out of the tombs a man with an unclean spirit, who had his dwelling among the tombs; and no one could bind him, not even with chains, because he had often been bound with shackles and chains. And the chains had been pulled apart by him, and the shackles broken in pieces; neither could anyone tame him. And always, night and day, he was in the mountains and in the tombs, crying out and cutting himself with stones.

When he saw Jesus from afar, and worshiped Him. And he cried out with a loud voice and said, "What have I to do with You, Jesus, Son of the Most High God? I implore You by God that You do not torment me."

For He said to him, "Come out of the man, unclean spirit!" Then He asked him, "What is your name?"

And he answered, saying, "My name is Legion; for we are many." (Mark 5:1–9)

Chris

October 2014

One of our coaches at our gymnastics school, Chris, was having trouble with a used car he had just bought. In six months, he had put $2,000 worth of repairs into the car. He took the car back at last and was told he didn't make enough money to trade it in on a newer or better car. Unless, they said, he could get his employer to state in a letter that he made more than his paystubs showed.

Chris told me about their requirement, and I told him, unfortunately, I think that's against the law and I could therefore not comply. Chris, being a devout Christian, said he understood and apologized for bringing his problems to me. I suggested we pray and see what God would have us do.

Later that day, I texted Chris and said, "The more I think about this, the more aggravated I get at what they suggested and how they will not help you!" Chris agreed and I said that perhaps he should find another witness and threaten to take them to the authorities.

Chris contacted his attorney who promptly followed up with the car dealer. Chris drove in to our parking lot the next day with a newer car, which had only 14,000 miles on it.

> But let your "Yes" be "Yes," and your "No," "No." For whatever is more than these is from the evil one. (Matt. 5:37)

Madison

November 2014

Saturday before Thanksgiving, Arty and I boarded a flight to Charlotte to visit Adam at his new place. We sat down beside a lovely young girl by the window. We struck up a conversation right away, and of course, I started sharing some of my "God" stories with her. We spent the whole three-hour flight talking as though we had known each other for a lifetime.

As our conversation unfolded, it turned out she came from a Christian family but had endured some setbacks in her life which had given her pause to doubt God's love for her. She was going to visit her mom and dad for Thanksgiving, but her connecting flight had been canceled, so the airline booked her another flight, and it just so happened that she was seated right next to me.

I don't know if Madison has made the full journey back into our Lord's loving arms, but I know the Holy Spirit was able to plant some seeds there that day, and I am sure he is still watering and nourishing them along her way.

I didn't know Madison before our trip to be praying for her, but I know a couple of people who are wearing the knees out of their jeans for her. Having been the parent of a couple of wayward kids myself, I know we sometimes blame ourselves that it must have been our fault or some neglect on our part that caused our children to wander. If Madison's parents ever read this chapter, I just want you to know, I think you did a fine job and raised a great kid.

> Being confident of this very thing, that He who has begun a good work in you will complete it until the day of Jesus Christ. (Phil. 1:6)

Booker

December 2014

Nine years ago, Adam bought a two-month-old Boxer. He named him Booker. A few years ago, when Adam decided he wanted to be a firefighter, he moved back in with us, along with Booker. We already had a black lab named Lexus. Then when Adam moved to Charlotte to begin his firefighting career, we inherited Booker full time since Adam had to spend four days at a time at the fire station and could not afford to hire someone to care for him.

Booker was a lovely dog. He drooled a lot, especially when he was standing over Lexus. The slobber would begin at the top of her head and slide down her back toward her tail as he lumbered through the room. He liked to shake his head and would sling spit all over the walls. Booker had a delicate digestive system, so Arty and I spent many hours cleaning up after him when his food did not agree with him. He loved to play with Lexus. Apparently, he got a little rough with her one day, because from that point onward, Lexus spent most of the time hiding under our office desk.

It is hard to believe, but Booker wormed his way into our hearts. When we would talk to him, he would stare at us with those great big brown eyes, cocking his head one way or the other. He followed me everywhere. Whenever I turned around, there he was, sitting or wagging his stump of a tail so hard his whole body shook.

On Thanksgiving of 2014, Arty and I traveled to Charlotte to visit with Adam and see his new townhome. We had a friend from church, Tyler, who house-sat and watched the dogs for us. Friday before we were due to return to Colorado, Tyler texted me saying he was worried about Booker. He was not eating. No matter how much Tyler coaxed Booker, he just would not eat. I replied back and told him not to worry. We would return and I would look after him then. I thought perhaps he was just missing us.

By the time we got back, Booker's ribs were more noticeable, and he looked drawn and sad. He would not lie down and just continually paced the floor. He would come up alongside me and lean on me. And he was still not eating. We watched him decline over the weekend, trying everything to get him to eat. We could tell he was miserable.

That Monday, I called the vet and she told me to bring Booker in. I rushed him up to the vet and explained to her what had gone on over the weekend. She wanted to keep him for tests while I went to my own doctor's appointment. I knew there was something serious going on, and I was also very concerned that the vet was going to say that she couldn't find anything. On my way home from my appointment, I prayed to God to make sure they wouldn't miss something and would be able to find out what was ailing poor Booker. At that time, I received a phone call from the vet who explained that they had taken an x-ray of Booker's abdominal area since his digestive system was what had always given him problems before. The technician had taken the x-ray a little too high and had accidentally caught the lower portion of Booker's lungs. The vet saw something peculiar and wanted to do an additional x-ray of his chest cavity so I immediately gave her permission.

When I arrived at the clinic, the vet took me in and showed me the x-rays. What she had seen when the technician accidentally took the x-ray was a mass that was filling a good portion of Booker's lungs. That was why he couldn't lie down. Poor Booker just couldn't breathe.

I wish we had a happy ending and could say that Booker was still with us, but the mass was inoperable. Booker was so miserable. Adam and I had to make the decision to put him down. Lexy drove down from Castle Rock and helped me.

Months afterward, I still miss that darned dog. I'd give anything to be able to clean up after him again.

> We glory in tribulations, knowing that tribulation produces perseverance; and perseverance, character; and character, hope. (Rom. 5:3–4)

Too Much Fun

December 2014

We always have a Christmas blowout for our staff at the gym. This Christmas, we took them to an ice rink and played broom ball. I tend to be very competitive and managed to stay on my feet until I was just standing there watching the action, and all of a sudden, my feet slid right out from under me, and I landed on my back and struck my head pretty hard on the ice. I jumped up right away and told all the youngsters I was fine. We enjoyed the rest of the night.

I didn't think too much of it until a week later when I started experiencing severe pain in the left side of my neck, dizziness, and fogginess. This worsened for a couple of days so I visited my chiropractor's office. She said I probably had a mild concussion and definitely a pretty bad case of whiplash. She treated me and sent me home, saying I should get checked out.

Instead, I went that night to church and had our pastor's son pray over me and anoint me with oil. By the next night, the symptoms had all disappeared completely.

Is anyone among you sick? Let him call for the elders of the church, and let them pray over him, anointing him with oil in the name of the Lord. And the prayer of faith will save the sick, and the Lord will raise him up. (James 5:14–15)

Covering My Mistakes

January 2015

A friend of ours lives in San Antonio, and her son's birthday was coming up. I figured Xen would be nine years old. We went to the store to find him a card. They had cards for every age except nine-year-olds. Go figure. We ended up buying a generic card instead.

When we arrived back at the house, I looked again at his date of birth and realized he was actually turning ten! Was it just a coincidence that the store didn't have a card for nine-year-olds? Or was it God's intervention.

> But it is good for me to draw near to God; I have put my trust in the Lord God, that I may declare all Your works. (Ps. 73:28)

God's Plans—Not Mine

March 2015

I woke up this Sunday morning, thanking God for a good night's rest for a change. It is so amazing how much better you feel when you can actually sleep!

I went downstairs to get ready for church when I began thinking to myself and talking to the Lord about the amazing opportunity he gave me writing this book and actually getting it published! My thoughts then turned to my friend who was just diagnosed with cancer. I began praying for her.

Then it occurred to me that I had reached a paradigm in my faith. It completely amazes me that I am writing a book that could reach a lot of people. How God might take an ordinary person like me to touch the lives of others, and that whatever is happening to me, good or bad, it's not about me. It's always about God. When I take off my self-centered glasses and put on God-centered glasses, all of a sudden whatever is happening to me becomes an opportunity to affect the lives of the people I come into contact with.

Will I be the bitter despondent Christian who can only tell people about the bad hand life has dealt me, causing the unbeliever to say, "If that's what being a Christian is about, I don't want to be one." Or am I going to meet my circumstances with a positive and hopeful attitude, with a smile and a hug for everyone around me no matter what, the way my good friend does? Am I going to be that Christian that when the unbeliever encounters me and my circumstance, they say, "I want what she has."

When I see through God's eyes, difficult circumstances just become another opportunity to see God's faithfulness, to build my faith, and to add another chapter to my book. When I understand it's about God using me to reach a dying world or to encourage another believer, everything changes.

As I sat down to read my Bible, I thought, *What an amazing book, God's Word.* Even when I don't feel like reading my Bible, I have to remember how much I have grown and changed and how people have come to me commenting on those changes that are so evident to others and I am oblivious to.

Then I thought, *We don't need mind-altering drugs. We need the Bible, the spirit-altering drug! Wow! That's good! I should write that down!* God then reminded me that I am writing a book.

Sunday mornings, Arty goes to church first service to help with Sunday school, and I stay home until the second service when we go to worship together. This particular Sunday, I had let my mind get the better of me, and now I was running late!

What made it worse was I was supposed to be there early to grab our favorite seats for Arty, myself, and our friend Bri. Also, this Sunday, my friend Christine was going to be at church, and she requested I save a seat for her. Christine had not been in church for several months because she had been attending church with her son. Christine is notoriously late for church.

When I finally was able to get in my car and proceed to the church, I did what I always do. I prayed and asked God to please cover me and help me get to church on time to get seats for everyone, or could he just not have anyone sit there? There I go again, putting God in a box and telling him how to do it. And gee, maybe God might want us to sit somewhere else.

I was still about five minutes away, not to mention the time it would take me to park and actually get into the sanctuary, when I received a call from Christine saying she was already at the church! I asked her to save us four seats.

Whew, that was close. As I continued on and approached and passed the intersection where I normally would have turned, I thought, *Wow, that's weird. I never go this way. Well, I wonder if God has a reason for me to go the back way to church.*

Sure enough, there was a lady with her car stuck in the ice in the gutter running across one of the side streets. A nice man was trying to push her car out, but it was stuck solidly in the rut. I quickly pulled over, put on my emergency flashers, and jumped out of my car to help them get her car out. Arty would be proud of me. I noticed right away that her front wheels were cranked, so I told her to straighten out her front wheels. The nice man and I had her car out in about five minutes.

If Christine had not been there to save our seats, I'm not sure I would have stopped to help. I'm ashamed to admit that my selfishness probably would have won that morning.

As I parked my car out on the street and began walking into the far entrance to the parking lot, which is on a fairly steep slope, another woman started going up the slope without enough speed to get her to the top. She was spinning her wheels in one spot while the long line of cars grew behind her. So I threw my Bible and purse onto the back of her car, her male passenger jumped out of the car, and we were able to get her car up and out of the way in no time flat.

When I got into the church and sat down beside Christine, I asked her why she was at Calvary instead of with her son. She said her son was out of town that weekend so she had decided not to make the long drive into her son's church.

> Remember not the former things, nor consider the things of old. Behold, I am doing a new thing; now it springs forth, do you not perceive it? I will make a way in the wilderness and rivers in the desert. (Isaiah 43:18–19)

Oh, How God Works When We Let Him

March 2015

In August 2014, I began putting together the answered prayers for this book. I had not kept a journal. Over the years, I could remember the really big answered prayers, the *whoa* moments. But I could not possibly remember the other incidental answered prayers that had occurred throughout my spiritual journey. So I prayed, "God, if you want me to write this book, then you will have to help me remember the answered prayers you want included."

As I sat down to handwrite my prayers, for each chapter, I started with a prayer for help. The words flowed from my fingertips without any effort. As I would write about one answered prayer, two or three more would come to mind, and I would jot down a note, *Oh, I have to remember to tell about that!*

As I was finishing up the final touches to my manuscript, I began to think a little more seriously about actually publishing my work. It had started as a lark, mostly just an exercise in personal therapy. But what if God actually wanted these stories out there? How would I go about doing that? I prayed again. I sought out the Internet and found several websites about self-publishing. Oh, my goodness. There was so much involved. I don't have the brainpower or the time to do all of that! So money isn't the object here. Getting the work done and in the hands of the people God wants it in is the main goal, so I'll check out some publishing houses.

I was drawn to Tate Publishing. They stated on their website that if you had submitted your manuscript to other publishers and had been rejected, they wanted to see it. But first, I thought I would have a couple of friends read the book and see what they had to say. Teresa read it and said she loved it and I should send it in. Jo said she thought it was too short and strangers probably would not be able to relate to the stories since they don't know me. But she suggested I submit the manuscript anyway.

I made a call to Tate Publishing and spoke with Ramie. She said she was pregnant and would love to read it as soon as she could. I told her I was not finished yet and would send it as soon as I could. A month later, in December, I sent her my finished manuscript, knowing in my heart that it probably would be rejected. But I had to try or I would always wonder.

I waited until January and had not heard anything, so I sent Ramie another e-mail asking if she had the chance yet to look at my manuscript. I received a call from Dr. Tate himself the next day explaining that Ramie had decided not to return after she had her baby and he was taking her clients until they could find a replacement for her. He asked me if I could resend my manuscript and I said that I would.

The next day I received another call from Dr. Tate who said he would love to publish my book! I held my cell phone away from my ear and looked at it incredulously for a moment, kind of like a tennis player looks at their racket when they miss a ball, like it's the racket's fault. I then returned the phone to my ear in total shock and said, "What?"

I have been living in a surreal kind of whirlwind throughout the production phase of this work. God must have plans that I am clueless about. He is at the helm and I am simply riding along on the poop deck. I don't know where he's going, but I am excited to be a part. During the editing stage, he continued to remind me of more prayers to add until the final manuscript was submitted.

Even this last chapter was directed by him. I started telling people of how a nobody came to be a published author. A couple of people said I should include this story in my book since it had been directed by God from the beginning. I started to write it but couldn't figure out where to place it chronologically. I gave up. The next day, I told one of our clients at the gym, Victoria, about the book. Without any prompting on my part, she said I should include this as the final chapter! When I am not receptive, God uses others to get his point across!

> A man's heart plans his way, but the Lord directs his steps. (Proverbs 16:9)

THE ROMAN ROAD

For whoever calls on the name of the Lord will be saved. (Rom. 10:13)

For all have sinned and fall short of the glory of God. (Rom. 3:23)

For the wages of sin is death, but the gift of God is eternal life in Christ Jesus our Lord. (Rom. 6:23)

For He made Him who knew no sin to be sin for us, that we might become the righteousness of God in Him. (2 Cor. 5:21)

That if you confess with your mouth the Lord Jesus and believe in your heart that God has raised Him from the dead, you will be saved. (Rom. 10:9–10)

You can pray like this:

Dear God, I confess I am a sinner and I am sorry. I need a Savior. I know I cannot save myself. I believe by faith that Jesus, your son, died on the cross to be my Savior. I believe he rose from the dead to live as my Lord. I turn from my sin and ask you, Lord Jesus, to forgive my sin and come into my heart. I trust you as my Savior and receive you as my Lord. Thank you, Jesus, for saving me.